T0339183

American Indian Lives

SERIES EDITORS

Kimberly Blaeser   ·
University of Wisconsin, Milwaukee

Brenda J. Child
University of Minnesota

R. David Edmunds
University of Texas at Dallas

K. Tsianina Lomawaima
Arizona State University

TOO STRONG
TO BE BROKEN

THE LIFE *of* EDWARD J. DRIVING HAWK

EDWARD J. DRIVING HAWK *and*
VIRGINIA DRIVING HAWK SNEVE

University of Nebraska Press | *Lincoln*

Library of Congress Cataloging-in-Publication Data
Names: Driving Hawk, Edward J., 1935- author. | Sneve, Virginia
Driving Hawk, author.
Title: Too strong to be broken: the life of Edward J. Driving
Hawk / Edward J. Driving Hawk, and Virginia Driving Hawk
Sneve.
Other titles: Life of Edward J. Driving Hawk
Description: Lincoln: University of Nebraska Press, [2020] |
Series: American Indian lives | Includes bibliographical
references.
Identifiers: LCCN 2020010789
ISBN 9781496222886 (hardcover)
ISBN 9781496223470 (epub)
ISBN 9781496223487 (mobi)
ISBN 9781496223494 (pdf)
Subjects: LCSH: Driving Hawk, Edward J., 1935- | Driving
Hawk, Edward J., 1935—Family. | Lakota Indians—Social life
and customs. | Disabled veterans—United States—Biography.
| Rosebud Sioux Tribe of the Rosebud Indian Reservation,
South Dakota—Politics and government. | Rosebud Indian
Reservation (S.D.) | Korean War, 1950-1953—Veterans—United
States—Biography. | Vietnam War, 1961-1975—Veterans—
United States—Biography. | Disabled veterans—United
States—Biography. | Rosebud Sioux Tribe of the Rosebud
Indian Reservation, South Dakota—Politics and government. |
Rosebud Indian Reservation (S.D.)
Classification: LCC E99.T34 D75 2020 |
DDC 362.4086/970092 [B]—dc23
LC record available at https://lccn.loc.gov/2020010789

Set in Lyon Text by Mikala R. Kolander.

CONTENTS

LIST OF ILLUSTRATIONS

AUTHOR'S NOTE

IN TELLING MY BROTHER'S STORY, I DREW GENEALOG-ical data from my 1995 publication *Completing the Circle*. These family facts show that Ed and I and our children are descendants of white men (mostly fur traders) who cohabited with or married Indian woman. We are proudly *Iyeska* (mixed blood), which means our families were and are acculturated, taking what is positive from white society and adapting it to Indian culture. Although our grandparents and parents were forced to attend boarding schools, our father, James Driving Hawk, stressed the importance of education for us to function in a modern world.

Our Indian ancestors became Christian to fill a desperate need described by Ella Deloria, whose father was one of the first Indian priests: "What good was it now anyway, in pieces? The sun dance—without its sacrificial core; festive war dances—without fresh war deeds to celebrate; the Hunka rite of blessing little children—without the tended Ring of Relatives to give it meaning—who would want such empty leavings?"

Our father was influenced by the Deloria conversion and by his grandmother, Lucy High Bear, who was a devout Christian. He also admired our mother's grandparents, the Reverend Charles Frazier and wife, Hannah, who became missionaries among the Sioux.

Ed and I are proud of our heritage.

Virginia

INTRODUCTIONS

Virginia

MY HUSBAND, VANCE, AND I WERE SAVORING THE WARM April day in Arizona, on a break from the damp chill of South Dakota. We were on the patio of my brother's home, chatting with him and his wife, Carmen, and reminiscing about our days on the Rosebud Reservation. We happily recalled childhood incidents, the sadness of our young father's passing, and our mother's resilience in raising us by herself. Ed recounted the highlights of his military career and his experiences as a tribal and national leader. As I listened to him, I realized that my brother had had many uncommon experiences in his life. He had been wounded in Korea, survived plane crashes and exposure to Agent Orange in Vietnam, was chairman of the Rosebud Sioux tribe, president of the National Congress of American Indians, operated several businesses, and was incarcerated for one year in a federal prison. He had survived many illnesses and surgeries due to Agent Orange and had had an amazing near-death experience. In addition, he was a family man—married to Carmen for sixty-three years, with whom he had raised four sons and a daughter. He was also a recovered alcoholic.

Today, Ed must use a wheelchair and is on oxygen because of the Agent Orange exposure. He reads, watches TV, and dozes in that chair, his chronic pain dulled by pills. Carmen said, "He needs something to do—to take his mind off his pain and handicap."

"Yeah," Ed agreed. "I'm turning into a vegetable."

After listening to his tales of the past, I suggested that he tell his life story, and he agreed. Thus, we began our collaboration on his story. I listened to the words he dictated on a recorder that typed them as he spoke. Then I transcribed his words into a readable narrative; first, his words in black ink, then my additions in red, which I then sent back to him to make sure all was okay. I made several trips to Arizona to interview him in order to clarify his recollections.

I had to research the Korean and Vietnam conflicts, military terminology and events, and Agent Orange. I checked facts about his experiences as chairman of the Rosebud Sioux tribe, where he participated in many traditional ceremonies and found out more about the National Congress of American Indians, which he presided over for two years. He also dealt with American presidents, congresspeople, and tribal leaders all over the United States.

I learned things about my brother that I had never known, and we are closer than we have ever been. I nearly wept as I wrote of how he lived through the horrors of war and his personal battle with alcohol. Grateful tears came as I recorded how Carmen was there for him—she supported him emotionally, physically, and financially through all those trying years; I marveled at how much they still loved each other. She is the main reason that he was too strong to be broken.

Edward

I have recorded my autobiography and my sister, Virginia Driving Hawk Sneve, has transcribed it into a readable narrative. I am proud to be a Lakota man and cherish the cultural heritage I gained from my parents and grandparents. I hope this recollection will let my descendants know and understand their heritage, which is part of who they are.

I am also proud of my military service in two wars, and proud of the time I gave to the Rosebud Sioux tribe and all tribal nations in the United States. But I am not proud of being an alcoholic and the years I wasted with booze. I hope my children and grandchildren can learn from my experiences and know that no matter how trying life can be—they can rise above it to be good people.

TOO STRONG TO BE BROKEN

1

Sonny

"I WAS FREEZING COLD, LIKE I WAS LYING ON A BED of ice; I hurt—agonizing pain all through my body. I opened my eyes and I saw myself on a gurney surrounded by doctors and nurses. I knew it was me, yet it wasn't—I hovered over the body and the operating room. I hurt so bad; I closed my eyes, willing the pain to end, then I began slowly and smoothly sliding into a tunnel of bright light and warmth. I was no longer cold, and the pain was gone; I felt relief and intense joy. I gazed into the light and saw Dad, Grandpa Driving Hawk, and an elder in a headdress I had never seen before, but I knew it was High Bear, my grandma's grandfather. Bill Menard, an old friend, was also there. I heard drums and Lakota men singing the old warrior song. The song faded, I saw Dad shake his head, the light dimmed—something pulled me away. With all my might I tried to stay, but the light faded, and some force pulled me back into the OR. I was sad—I wanted to stay with my elders in that warm and safe place."

This was the vision, or near-death experience, that made Ed realize his elders, Lakota spirits, had always been with him, even though he was unaware of their protection, through calamities, near disasters, and his own self-destructive behavior. They were the reason he wasn't killed in war and how he survived the effects of Agent Orange. It was that toxic chemical, which caused cancer in one kidney, that had led to surgery and this amazing vision. Ed believed the spirits helped him endure even though he wasn't conscious of their presence.

Until that vision, he had never given a thought to being Lakota, with the tribe's unique spirituality and values. As a boy he was surrounded by *tiyospaye*, an extended family that was a vital part of the Lakota's value system and included elders no longer with us. He recalled feeling loved and protected by those around him.

He was born March 4, 1935, at the Indian Health Service (IHS) infirmary at the Rosebud boarding school in Mission, South Dakota, two years after his sister, Virginia. His father was James Henry Driving Hawk, son of Robert Driving Hawk and Flora Clairmont Driving Hawk. His mother was Rose Edna Ross, daughter of Edward Owen Ross and Harriet Howe Frazier.

Rose and Jimmy met at the Bureau of Indian Affairs (BIA) boarding school in Mission, South Dakota. The school was one of the many such schools established by the federal government in the United States in the 1880s. The schools' purpose was to assimilate Indians into the mainstream culture, starting with removing children from home at a young age to keep them from the "negative" Indian ways. They were educated in basic English reading and writing skills and forbidden to speak "Indian," and they were converted to Christianity and thus were "civilized." They stayed at school until they had finished the equivalent of the eighth grade.

Jimmy knew very little English when he enrolled since Lakota was spoken at home. His grandfather was named Chanskan nah ho pah, which was translated as Driving Hawk by agency officials, with his first name listed as Jacob. When the Indians moved to reservations, government officials devised a way to classify members of the same family. Prior to this time, each person had an individual name, with no surname. Now the father's name became the last name for the wife and children and first names were assigned from an alphabetical list. Thus it was Jacob Driving Hawk with his wife listed as Mrs. Driving Hawk, but Robert referred to her as Ina, Lakota for "mother."

He had no recollection of her as she died when he was a child. He and his sister Virginia were raised by Jacob's second wife.

Robert attended the Indian School at Chamberlain, South Dakota, where he met Flora Clairmont. Her grandfather was a French fur trader, Henri Clairmont, who married Emily Trapan, and who fathered James Clairmont. James in turn wed Pejuta Okawin, who was the first to be baptized "Lucy" at Saint John's Episcopal Chapel. This was near where her brother, Can Gleska Wakinyan's *tiyospaye* were settled on the Rosebud Reservation. Lucy, who did not go to school and spoke only Lakota, had no conflict as a Lakota medicine woman who healed with herbs and plants while praying to Wakantanka, the Christian god, as she smudged a patient with sacred smoke of burning sage.

Lucy's father was Mato Wakantuya, High Bear, and Skanskwin, the first to be confined to the reservation after High Bear fought Custer's troops at the Battle of the Little Big Horn.

James Driving Hawk was a mixed-blood descendant of white men and Indian women, and no English was spoken in his home. He recalled what a tough time it was adapting to a strange society, let alone learning the peculiarities of English speech.

"You won't do that again, will you?" a teacher asked. "Yes," answered the child. The teacher punished the child, unaware of what the child meant. One said "yes" to a question like this, when in English the answer should be "no." English says, "No, I will not," while the Indian child says "Yes," meaning "you are right that I will not."[1]

Jimmy mastered reading English faster than he did speaking. Rose recalled that because of the trouble Jimmy had learning in a strange language, he made sure that English was Ed and Virginia's first language. That helped them when they were in school, but as adults they regretted their lack of fluency in Lakota.

Rose had different problems with language. Because she and her siblings spoke only English and little Lakota, they were scorned and cruelly teased by Lakota-speaking students, called "fake Indians" or "wannabe whites." Rose's mother, Harriet, was of Santee Dakota, Ponca, and Scot and French descent. Her grandmother was Ehamani, sister of chief Red Wing who cohabited with John Frazier, son of Scots fur trader James Frazer from Canada. John stayed neutral during the 1862 Minnesota uprising and aided white settlers in escaping the wrath of Dakota warriors who rebelled against corrupt white traders who confiscated their rations and abused their women.

After the uprising was quelled, fourteen warriors were hanged at Mankato and most other Santee were evicted to Dakota Territory. John could stay but could only keep one wife and her children; the second wife and family were sent away. His son Charles was born to Ehamani, christened Margaret, on the way to Dakota Territory.

Margaret was under the protection of her brother and later moved with them to Santee, Nebraska. All of them converted to Christianity and learned English and the children were educated at Riggs Institute, a school operated by Presbyterian and congregational missionaries. Her son Charles became a Congregational missionary with his wife, Hannah, who was a descendant of Englishman John Howe and Lucille Leclaire.

Rose; her sister, Alma; and brother, George, completed the eighth grade at Rosebud then attended the Santee Normal Training School in Santee, Nebraska. It was also a boarding school, located on the bluffs of the Missouri River, but did not have the military strictness of the government schools. It was run by the Presbyterian Church, where students were first taught in their native tongue until they learned English. Rose's mother had been educated at Santee and urged her children to attend the school.

Rose and Jimmy's romance began at Rosebud, and he followed her to Santee. He had first planned to finish high school at the Haskell Institute in Lawrence, Kansas, which was founded in 1884 and operated by the BIA as a boarding school for Indian students from all over the nation.[2] However, Jimmy was so in love that he chose to go to Santee.

George and Jimmy graduated from Santee and their parents were there for the commencement ceremonies. Rose rode with her parents to their home in Okreek, a small village on the Rosebud Reservation. Jimmy and his parents went to Mission and Jimmy got a job on a local ranch. When he had money, Jimmy borrowed his father's Model A and went to Okreek to see Rose. One time, he persuaded her to go for a ride with him that turned into a weeklong jaunt. They first drove to White River then on to Crow Creek (about ninety miles away on the Missouri River), then, out of gas and money, they hitched a ride Rose's to Uncle George Frazier's home. George was Rose's uncle and a doctor with the IHS, and the family called him "Uncle Doctor." He told the runaways that both sets of their parents had been looking all over for them. "Well," recalled Rose, "by the time we got to Uncle Doctor's, it was too late"— she thought she was pregnant.

Uncle Doctor sent word to Mission that the runaways were safe; he fed them, gave them gas money, and told them to go straight home. They got back to Okreek and found both sets of parents and Father Barbour (the Episcopal priest) waiting for them. Arrangements were made for a hasty wedding on May 26, 1932. Such a scandal—but the young couple were happy.

They lived in a small one-room house that Robert Driving Hawk built for them in Mission, South Dakota. The small prairie village had been named after the Episcopal missionaries established Saint Mary's school for Indian girls and Hare school for Indian boys in the 1870s. Mission was then a thriving town of a thousand residents with Abrouzek's general store, a Phillips 66 gas station, a bar, hardware store, the *Todd County Tribune* office, a Roman Catholic church and Trinity Episcopal Church, and a jail.

The Ross and Driving Hawk families were the second generation of Lakota who were Christian and devout Episcopalians.

Rose became an organist and Jim had been an altar boy for Father Barbour. The priest encouraged Jim to be more active as a helper in the church. A helper was a layman trained to read morning prayer on Sundays and work with church members in the community; it was the first step toward ordination to the priesthood.

Jim had not gone to college but had had a theological education by studying the Ashley House Course. The course was designed by the venerable Edward Ashley, archdeacon for the church in South Dakota. He recognized that Sioux candidates for ordination did not have the usual college preparation but were trained to work in the reservation churches.[3] This made it possible for native men to complete a study for ordination without leaving the reservation. Jim's mentor during the course was Father Paul Barbour of Mission; he was also the superintending presbyter of all the Episcopal priests and churches on the Rosebud Reservation.

While in Mission, Rose discovered she was pregnant and expecting the baby around April 1, 1933—though she hoped it wouldn't be an April Fool's baby. She had an easy pregnancy until the night of February 20, when her pains began—too early. It was a wild night with winds whipping the snow into drifts. It was a twenty-mile gravel road to the IHS in Rosebud. The gravel road was a challenge for their old Model A on sunny days, and Jimmy did not want to chance it in a blizzard. He bundled Rose into the car and headed to the boarding school's infirmary five miles from Mission. He knew there was a resident nurse who cared for the children and staff of the school and hoped she could deliver the baby. It was twenty minutes through the blizzard, and he was relieved to find not only the nurse when they arrived, but also the agency doctor, who had been stranded by the storm. An hour later Virginia was born, a squalling three-pound preemie. The doctor cautioned the young parents about the survival odds for such a tiny baby without an incubator and other hospital facilities. The nurse heated the stove in her quarters, left the door open to cool, then placed the swaddled handful into the warm oven. Years after hearing this story, Edward told Virginia, "Now we know why you're half-baked."

Two years later, Edward was born at the same infirmary in similar weather conditions, but he was a sturdy seven pounder and a happy, healthy baby, and his family called him Sonny to differentiate him from his grandfather, after whom he was named. An aunt told later told him that she thought he was actually called "Sunny" because of his carefree, happy nature.

After Sonny's birth the family moved to Ponca Creek, where Jimmy was assigned to be the helper at All Saints Chapel. It was part of the Milk's Camp community south of Herrick, South Dakota, which got its name from Chief Osampi, whose name translated to "milk" and whose band camped along the creek and settled there in 1889 when the Sioux reservations were established. The community was in a green, tree-shaded area above the creek and was made up of the BIA day school for elementary students before they went to boarding school, a warehouse for commodity goods for the people, a large garden, and a cannery building where the garden produce was preserved. The chapel was about two miles upstream, near the creek, and the family's first home was a two-room house. The main room was the kitchen, with a large wood-burning iron stove on which Rose cooked and which also heated the house. The family slept in the second room.

On the first night the family spent in their new home, baby Sonny's bed was the top drawer of a dresser. Rose heard him fussing and got up to find that he was covered with red bedbug bites. She changed his clothes and soothed the itch as best she could and took him into the iron double bed. Virginia's bed was a cast iron crib and safe from the bugs. After that Jimmy rigged a hammock that hung from metal hooks in a corner and Ed slept well. Rose told Mrs. Barbour about the bugs and she sent them a sulfur candle, which burned all day. The fumes killed the pests while the family stayed outdoors but left a rotten egg odor in the rooms.

The children had no other playmates but got along well together and had fun playing with their few toys outdoors when the weather permitted or under the kitchen table when it didn't.

Jim's helper wage was fifteen dollars a month, so he had to work additional jobs to support his family. One of the jobs he had was with the Works Progress Administration (WPA), which was part of Franklin Roosevelt's New Deal policy to provide jobs for the unemployed during the Depression. He worked on a dam about ten miles away. Every day he would get up early and walk to work, do his job, and walk back. Sonny would sit on a post at the far end of the fenced yard, waiting for Jim to return, because "Dad always saved a bit from his lunch bucket for a treat for while we walked to the house."

One day Jim came back with some frog legs, which one of the other workers, Buster Catchall, had given him. Rose cooked them, and it was a feast day at the house. Sonny said the frog legs tasted as good as chicken. According to Buster, there had been a cold snap that had happened so quickly that the water froze as frog jumped into the dam, leaving legs sticking out of the ice so that all Buster had to do was snap up all he could carry. It was a good story, but Sonny often wondered if that was the way it really happened.

Jim had other jobs as well and traveled all the way to Wyoming to cut fence posts along with the other Indian men working for the WPA. He was gone for many months—it seemed that he was away forever, and the children greatly missed their father.

Another job he had was playing in a band called Crazy Horse and the Syncopators. He had learned to play the clarinet and trombone for a marching band when he was a student at the Rosebud boarding school and was a talented musician. He played with an Indian friend on drums and one other who was the banjo picker in the group. The band played for dances on

Friday and Saturday nights in small towns on and off the reservation. On one occasion Rose and the children went with him; they sat inside listening to the music until Rose took the children out to the car where they slept until the dance was over. Jimmy collected his fee, and they went home. Ed recalled that it was exciting to be away from home and up so late—it felt like a holiday.

Jimmy also sang. He was a tenor and he and three other men in the Milk's Camp community formed a barbershop quartet. They met in the rectory and the children recalled falling asleep to the tight melodic harmonies they sang.

Rose was musical, too, thanks to the piano lessons her mother, Harriet—who had learned from missionaries—gave her. Rose played the organ for church services and would sit Sonny and Virginia in the front pew beside the organ. When she began a hymn, the congregation would stand to sing. One time, when Sonny was about four years, he crawled under the pews and all the way out the back door. No one stopped him, just smiled and stepped aside to let him by. "I really got scolded for doing that and never did it again."

The Driving Hawks had a dog at Ponca Creek, Soup, a German shepherd mix. Villages always had many dogs in camp, a holdover from nomadic times when the dogs could alert a camp to an enemy approach or be trained to pull a small travois loaded with household goods when moving camp. In times of poor game hunts, however, these same dogs fed the village, which was why Soup was given her name.

Soup was big trusty dog who played catch and chased the children and was a good friend to Sonny. She was also a smart dog and Rose sent her with the children when the two went out to play in the prairie. When it was time to come home, Mom blew a whistle and Soup would bark and herd them back. One day she had thirteen pups and there was no way to feed them after they quit nursing, so Jimmy gave them away. Sonny overheard the grown-ups discussing the puppies' destiny—puppy soup. Sonny was alarmed and frightened for the pups—he didn't want them killed and certainly not eaten. The next Sunday the people who wanted the puppies arrived in their wagon and Sonny heard them say they wanted to take the puppies home with them. Sonny wanted to save the puppies, so he took them and Soup, crawled under the church, and stayed there. Virginia knew where he was but said nothing as Jimmy, Rose, and other adults came out of church and looked all over for the dogs and then realized Sonny was gone too. He tried to keep the pups quiet, but they yipped, and Jimmy found him. Before taking the pups, the new owners said they would not eat them. Sonny never found out if the pups became a meal.

Soup was a loyal dog. Once the Driving Hawks visited Rose's parents' home in Okreek, which was about seventy miles from Ponca Creek. They stayed about a week, and when it was time to go home, they were amazed to see Soup coming down the lane to the Ross home—she had traveled the whole seventy miles following the scent of car tires. Sonny was so glad to see her—and she got a ride home.

The next year they again went Okreek, but just out of the yard, Sonny looked back and spotted Soup trotting along after as if she knew where she was going. Jimmy stopped the car and Soup jumped up and down, wagged her tail and Sonny picked her up and held her all the away to Okreek. No doubt she would have kept walking if Sonny hadn't seen her. Sadly, Soup was run over by a car in Okreek after the family moved there when Jimmy transferred from Ponca Creek.

Jimmy was often gone from home to work and earn money to support his family. This was during the Depression and things were tough for everybody. On Friday nights, the family drove to the little town of Napier, Nebraska—six or seven miles from Ponca Creek. Local farmers, who had no feed for their chickens, brought them to town and threw them off the back of their trucks for anyone to catch. Jimmy and Sonny ran out into the street and caught one and happily took it home. It was a scrawny bird and Rose decided to fatten it up before butchering it to eat. She tethered it by a string to a stake in the yard where it could get grasshoppers and leftover scraps she fed it. After several weeks, before Jimmy left for his job he told Rose that he thought the bird was fat enough to have for supper. He sharpened the ax before he left.

Rose made the children sit on the porch steps out of the way and she led the chicken to a stump, grabbed its legs, and swung its head against the wood, hoping to knock the chicken out before she decapitated it. The chicken was stunned, but as Rose lay its head on the stump and raised the ax, the bird clucked and jumped up and ran. Soup barked and joined Rose and the children in chasing the chicken until Sonny caught it. "I'll hold it, Mom," he offered, but Rose made him stay with Virginia on the steps. She tried again and once more the chicken got away. Finally, it lay senseless on the stump and Rose swung the ax, the bird's head dropped to the ground, but its body flopped around, spraying blood all over the yard. "Now what?" Rose yelled and the children thought she was laughing, but then to their horror they realized she was weeping. Sonny thought the bird had hurt her after it finally fell to the ground because there was blood on her arms and her dress. "At supper," he recalled, "I really liked the chicken and Dad told Mom how good it was, but she didn't eat a bite of it."

Another time in Napier, Jimmy saved money to buy some ice cream cones. That was the first ice cream the children ever had and to this day Sonny recalls that none has ever tasted as good as that first lick.

Rose was resourceful in providing food while Jimmy was gone and worked in the Milk's Camp community vegetable garden and helped harvest and can the vegetables. Donald Ross, Rose's youngest brother, came from Okreek to help Rose take care of the children while she worked at the garden and cannery. All of the workers picked bushels of cucumbers and put them into big vats to make pickles. Everybody was busy and having a good time when someone looked up and yelled, "Tornado!"

Everyone dropped what they were doing and ran for shelter in the low areas along the creek. Rose called the children and Donald threw them into the car and he jumped onto the running board as Rose sped off in the old Model A toward home. Donald hung on to the rattling and shaking car—it had never been driven so fast. The children huddled silent and frightened in the back seat until the car skidded to a stop and they all ran to the root cellar. Rose and Donald struggled to lift the heavy wooden door and then pull it shut after all were inside. It was a dark, gloomy, spiderwebby, musty-smelling hole and they could hear the wind howling and loose items banging about above therm. "Soup, Soup!" Sonny cried, "we gotta get Soup!"

"We can't!" yelled Rose. The children could barely hear her over the roaring gusts pulling at the cellar door.

They huddled in the dark among cobwebs and mice droppings until, as suddenly as it had begun, the wind stilled, and they heard Soup barking. She was okay. They never did find out how she had sheltered, but she was safe.

They came out of the cellar and there was very little damage—the house was intact, with only the washtub blown off the porch into the yard. They were all relieved and Sonny hugged his dog.

The Milk's Camp community garden grew sugarcane, and Rose and other workers helped make molasses. Everyone who worked at the garden and cannery got a share of the final product. In addition to that, Rose also had a small garden at home where she raised potatoes, carrots, onions, and tomatoes. Every day she pumped buckets of water from the well (they had neither indoor plumbing nor electricity) and carried them to water the plants. As the potato plants got bigger, bugs chewed on them and it was Virginia and Sonny's job to pick them and put them in a coffee can of kerosene.

One year locusts were so thick on the ground one couldn't walk without stepping on them. They were about four inches long and as big around as a one-inch pipe. They ate everything and stripped the garden to bare sticks on the ground and there was no alfalfa in any of the fields. There was nothing green in the area—just stems. At night when the temperature cooled, the locusts lit on the warm west side of the house and church. Rose and Jimmy got brooms and swatters, smashed the locusts and killed hundreds of them. They were the enemy. Then one morning they lifted up into a tight dark swarm and were gone as quickly as they had come.

"Those bugs left only sticks in my corn," complained an old German man who farmed a ways down the creek—their nearest neighbor. He was a bachelor, probably in his sixties who always wore the same blue shirt and overalls and rarely bathed. About once a week he would stop his team and wagon and holler at the house with cans of fresh milk and newly laid eggs in the wagon bed. Rose and the children would carry clean quart jars to the wagon and trade home-baked bread for fresh milk and eggs. When the Driving Hawks went to Herrick, they stopped see if he wanted to go along. He climbed into the back seat with Sonny and Virginia who cringed away from him because of his odor. He sat there and answered "*ja*" or "*nein*" to Rose's question. He acted as if he were driving a horse, "Git, git git up." Then "whoa now," when the car stopped at the gate. As soon as the car drove through and the gate closed, he tsked "git up" again. Ed remembers Rose looking back and smiling at the old gentle man.

Ed recalled that Virginia began school at the Milk's Camp day school when she was five because the BIA-run school needed one more student to stay open and feed them a noon meal. Two years later Eddie started first grade and Jimmy during nice weather walked with them the two miles to school and often carried Sonny when he tired on the way home. In rain or cold winter, he cranked up the Model A and drove them.

He always told them that school was important and that they should always attend no matter what.

In the winter Jimmy chopped wood to burn in the kitchen range, which kept the house warm and on which Rose prepared meals. Soup always went with him into the woods and one day the dog came home alone. She barked, whined, and pulled at Rose's dress until Rose finally understood Soup was telling her that something was wrong. She put Virginia and Sonny in bed and told them to stay there until she got back, and followed the dog to the creek.

She found Jimmy sitting in the snow, bleeding from a gash in his scalp. The ax-head had come off as he swung it and hit him in the head. Rose managed to get him home, where she bathed the wound, bandaged it with a dish towel, and got the barely conscious Jimmy into the car. She dressed the children, put on their coats, and wrapped them in quilts in the back seat and drove to find help for Jimmy.

Virginia has dim memories of holding on to her wailing brother, who wanted to sit on his father's lap. She was frightened and cold, even though she and Sonny were snuggled under quilts. The next thing she remembers was Grandpa Ross lifting her out of the car. Rose had driven seventy miles to Okreek in the car with no heater, praying the whole way that she could do it and that Jimmy would be okay. The children stayed with Grandma Ross while Grandpa Ross went with Rose to the Rosebud IHS hospital. Jim had a concussion and had to have several stitches in his scalp and the children sensed Rose's concern when she told them, "Dad has to stay in the hospital for a few days." Virginia worried that her father would not come home and cried happy tears when he did, and he showed them the stitches in his head.

The children heard this story many times while they were growing up and Rose shivered as she retold it when she was ninety-five. "I'd never been so scared. It was so cold. I prayed the whole way that the car wouldn't break down. I guess I could have taken Jimmy to the doctor in Bonesteel" (twenty miles distant) "but I wanted to get home." As adults Virginia and Ed marveled at their brave mother who drove all that way in the winter to save their father.

It was a tough existence at Ponca Creek, but the Driving Hawks were happy, giving Sonny and Virginia secure love.

After Jimmy was out of the hospital, he resumed his duties as helper in Ponca Creek. He not only held morning prayer every Sunday, but he and Rose were also the janitors who cleaned and set up the altar. Once a month Father Barbour came and held a communion service with Jimmy assisting. The diocesan bishop, Blair Roberts, visited once a year for confirmation. Sonny looked forward to the bishop's visits because Rose always made a dish with biscuits over the top—it was so good. When Rose made it, he always knew the bishop was coming. So he called the dish "Bishop Roberts Stew."

Jimmy was transferred from Ponca Creek to Okreek when Virginia was nine and Sonny seven. Okreek was a small Indian village along the creek, with oak trees that flamed red in the fall. This was the first reservation home for Chief Good Voice's *tiyospaye*, who set up tepees in family groups along the creek. The BIA trained the men to build log cabins where their tepees once stood scattered up and down both sides of the creek. When the Driving Hawks lived there in the 1940s, most of the cabins were replaced with wood-framed houses, but there was no running water or electricity in the Indians' homes.

The Episcopal Church had built a rectory down the hill from Calvary Chapel. Ed recalled that "The Okreek house was a mansion! It had a living room with a coal stove and piano. I could run in a circle through the whole house from the living room through the kitchen and two bedrooms and back to the living room." There was no running water or electricity, but he recalled playing cards by the light of an Aladdin lamp. The outhouse was in the back with a storage shed nearby and the yard was fenced to keep out wandering horses and cattle.

While in Okreek, Jimmy was ordained a deacon and his family were all proud of him. In 1941, after Pearl Harbor, he tried to enlist in the army like other young men, but his physical exam revealed a stomach tumor and the army would not take him. That tumor later became cancerous and he had several operations in Sioux Falls and even one at the Mayo Clinic in Rochester, Minnesota.

Every day during the war the family listened to the battery-powered radio for news of the overseas battles, especially for places local boys were fighting. Sonny's uncles saw battle: Leo in the navy, George in the Seabees in the Pacific, and Harvey fought with the army in Europe. Sonny and his pals played soldier—not cowboys and Indians. They dug foxholes, built forts, and fought against imaginary Nazis because no one wanted to pretend to be one. Sonny always said he would be a soldier when he grew up.

In Okreek, Deacon James had many duties besides holding services. He was often called to intervene in domestic disagreements and other quarrels. Once he had to a stop a fight between two women who were screaming, hair pulling, kicking, and biting each all over the road—fighting over Ollie Wright.

Ollie was one of many interesting characters in Okreek who impressed Sonny because even though he was Indian, he was the epitome of a colorful Western cowboy. He was tall, handsome, with a big hat, wore chaps and spurs, and had a way with the women. He was also a well-to-do rancher. After World War II he and other Indian veterans were each allotted twenty head of cattle cobranded with the BIA initials and a personal brand to start their own ranching operations. Most of the other veterans traded their cows to Ollie for a bottle of whiskey or two, so he ended up with all the cattle. When the BIA cattle had calves, they belonged to the local rancher, so Ollie managed to corner the cattle market on the east side of the reservation.

On the other side of the reservation, Joe Waln was another colorful rancher. He did all the things cowboys should do, including ride broncs in rodeos. His nickname was Joe "Bad" Waln, a well-turned-out man, good looking, and also a lady's man. Ed tried imitating the cowboy's casual swagger with fingers hooked into his belt loops but remembered he didn't get it right "because I didn't have cowboy boots."

After the war Sonny and other boys admired the WWII vets. "They were our heroes," Ed recalled, and they wanted to be just like them. There was no alcohol allowed on the reservation, but the vets were used to getting it in the service and now they bought it from bootleggers on the reservation—who even sold it to underage kids. "Drinking," Ed said, "was a manly thing to do."

Sonny and Virginia walked a half mile to the Okreek day school, but every day on the way Carolyn Flood, an older, bigger student, would stop, push them around, and take their lunch. She was a bully. This went on until Sonny talked about her to Grandpa Ross, who told him, "If you punch those bullies right in the nose—they'll bleed and run right off." The next day as they walked to school, Carolyn showed up as usual. Sonny said, "Watch this," and he slugged her in the nose and blood splattered all over. She screamed, yelled, and ran off. After that, Sonny and Virginia safely walked all the way to school. Carolyn never bothered them again.

Years later, when Sonny moved back to the reservation after he got out of the air force, he visited Uncle Cleveland Clairmont, who proudly said, "I want you to meet my girlfriend, Carolyn Flood." There she was, the bully from Okreek. She had grown up to be an attractive woman—and his uncle's sweetheart.

Virginia was a skinny small girl and was often picked on by bigger girls. One time walking home she wept because a mean older girl bopped her on the head with a book. "She took my pencils and called me 'little shit,'" Virginia told Sonny.

"Punch her in the nose," Eddie said.

"She's bigger than me," Virginia cried. Sonny thought a

bit then said, "Pinch her. Grab a tiny pinch of skin and twist it hard—then run."

The next time the meanie raised her arm to bop Virginia, the little girl quickly grabbed a tiny pinch under her enemy's arm. The meanie screamed, and Virginia ran. That meanie never again got close enough to hit, but still called Virginia names. Virginia tried not to let it bother her.

At Christmas, men from the Okreek church went to an area near Valentine, Nebraska, about fifty miles south, where tall cedars grew. Eddie, ten, rode along in the back of the truck with Jimmy and other men. He had to stay in the truck while the men found the right tree, cut it down, and loaded it, and rode home amid the scratchy branches and sweet aroma of the fresh-cut cedar. It was set up in the guild hall, where the women decorated it with tinsel and construction paper chains the Sunday school children had made. White handkerchiefs also trimmed the tree—one for each adult and a toy for each child, who also received a paper bag with an apple, peanuts, and hard candy. Ed remember seeing a football tied high on the tree and hoping it was for him. "It seemed like it was forever before my name was called and I got the ball."

The next Christmas he had measles and had to stay home. "I hated to miss the Christmas pageant and tree and gifts. I couldn't stand it and finally ran over to the hall. When I got in the door, everyone scattered until Mom took me back to the house. I still got a present, but maybe I gave my measles away."

Eddie remembered another ride in a truck. In June all the South Dakota Indian Episcopalians gathered for an annual Niobrara convocation, so named after the river that ran on the South Dakota–Nebraska border and what the first Episcopal bishop of the region called his territory. The Niobrara convocation was hosted each year by a different reservation. The gathering was similar to prereservation meetings where the bands camped in a traditional circle for ceremony, hunts, and social dances where young people courted among unrelated *tiyospayes*. Now, at modern church convocations, two to three hundred people no longer had horse and wagon to travel in. Big farm trucks were loaded with families along with their tents, bedding, and cooking utensils to travel sometimes hundreds of miles. It was often a hot slow trip and the riders often passed the time singing hymns in Lakota.

At the convocation site, located near the largest reservation chapel, delegates and families set up camp in designated sites for each reservation—Rosebud, Pine Ridge, Standing Rock, Cheyenne River, Sisseton, Yankton, Lower Brule, and Crow Creek. Like the way their ancestors had in sites for the seven council fires of Sicangu, Ogalalas, Hunkapa, Minneonjou, Sihasapa, Oohennumpa, Itazipo, and Yankon.

As in the old days, an *eyapaha*, camp crier, was named to serve the four-day gathering. Ed recalled "I was so proud when Grandpa Driving Hawk was chosen and I followed him as he walked through the camp announcing the times and places for the men's, women's, and youth meetings as well as other important activities.

"I liked convocation. There was lots to eat, fun games for the kids. I got to get together with friends like Teddy Roulliard, my lifelong friend, whose dad was also an Episcopal priest."

Sometimes the gathering, held in late June, coincided with bad weather. Ed recalls a dark night when Jimmy roughly grabbed him and put him and Virginia in the car and told her to take care of her brother. Thunder roared and severe lightning lit a nightmare scene of tents being pulled from the ground and desperate men trying to hold them down. "I was petrified," Ed recalled, "and tried to get out of the car, but Virginia made me stay." Finally, the storm ended, the tent was still there, but all the bedding and clothing were a sodden mess; and the whole family spent the rest of the night in the car.

Otherwise, life in Okreek was a good one for the Driving Hawks. The house was large enough for the children to have their own rooms. They had playmates and liked school. Father

Barbour and his wife, Margaret, were supportive of the newly ordained priest and often visited the family. They invited the Driving Hawks to a dinner at their rectory home in Mission. Sonny fussed about having to bathe in the middle of the week in addition to the usual Saturday scrubbing. The family all dressed like they were going to a Sunday service. At the Barbours' the table was covered with linen cloth and napkins with china dishes, silver utensils, and tall candles lit in the center. It was a new dining experiences for the Driving Hawks.

Jimmy had told Sonny, "You sit up straight, don't chew with your mouth open and watch Father Barbour—eat like he does."

Sony watched closely and took a bite or drank from a crystal glass when Father Barbour did. The priest soon noticed what the boy was doing and put the soupspoon down then lifted the bowl and drank. So did Sonny. No one around the table said a word.

The Barbours were concerned when Jimmy became ill and was diagnosed with stomach cancer. They helped with the expenses of Jimmy and Rose traveling to Sioux Falls, South Dakota's largest city, for the several surgeries.

While Rose and Jimmy were away, the children stayed with Grandma and Grandpa Ross. They fondly remember the time with their grandparents. But they didn't know how sick their father was.

Grandma and Grandpa Ross were special persons in their lives, but that summer in 1945 they became more so because the children missed their parents so much. Grandpa Edward (after whom Sonny was named) was born during the blizzard of 1908 at Rosebud Butte, Dakota Territory. His mother, Mary DuBray, was a resourceful, strong woman who kept her family clothed, fed, and clean despite the adversities of reservation life. She was one of a few women who drove an automobile and often traveled alone while Joseph was busy with ranch chores. She had to go to the Spotted Tail Agency (later renamed Rosebud) for the monthly distribution of commodities when a blizzard hit, and the car stalled in the blinding snow. She felt labor pains and she delivered the baby all by herself. A passerby fortunately found the mother and child and drove them home. A frantic Joseph was relieved that it all turned out okay and it was an often-told family story about the strong little woman.

Edward helped farm at the farm on the Keyapha River near Clearfield, South Dakota, but then decided to attend Columbus College in Chamberlain, South Dakota, later named the Chamberlain Indian School, which was equivalent to a high school course. But after his father died, Edward quit school to help his mother care for his younger brother and two sisters and manage the farm. After he married Harriet Frazier, the first marriage recorded in Tripp County, they cared for his mother while they raised four sons and five daughters, of whom Rose, Sonny's and Virginia's mother, was the second oldest.

Edward Ross was no saint and had a weakness for a nip of whiskey when he could get it. He and his brother-in-law Earl Frazier were arrested for bootlegging (alcohol was banned on reservation land), but only Edward was convicted. He served one year in the South Dakota State Penitentiary. During that year Harriet's father, Charles Frazier, arranged for Harriet and her four children to live in a small one-roomed house in Winner, South Dakota. Rose started school in Winner. She remembers that she took a doll dress her mother had made to school for show and tell. It had been a bleak Christmas without Edward at home.

After Edward served his sentence, the family moved back along the Keyapaha River into a house Ed had built on his allotted land. This land was his under the Dawes Act, which Congress had passed in 1887. Each head of family received one-quarter (160 acres) section of land and each single person over eighteen was given one-eighth (80 acres) of a section. The purpose of the act was to break up reservation land into smaller allotments in hopes that an Indian would be responsible for it, raise crops, and gradually learn to support himself and his family so that they would assimilate into general society. The government would protect individual property rights but would no longer have to support them.[4]

Edward farmed his land, which was in fertile ground near the Keyapha River and produced good crops. Still, cash was tight, and in addition to farming he hauled freight with a team of horses and wagon from Winner to Valentine. Harvey and Olive were born there, and Rose became the caregiver for the baby, whom she toted around on her hip. Years later, as an adult, when she was pregnant with Virginia, Uncle Doctor told her that the curvature of her spine was probably the result of toting Olive and her younger brothers and sisters on her hip, which had misaligned her still-growing spine.

After the birth of another baby, Leo, Harriet was sick in bed and Rose was her caregiver and little mother to her younger siblings. In the afternoon when Harriet was resting, the children would play in the shallow waters of the Keyapaha. Olive splashed in a little water near the bank and watched the others wade and frolic in the stream. Rose recalled, "I kept an eye on Olive, but the next time I looked, all I saw was the top her head and her waving hands above the water." The sand had washed out from under the baby and she was helplessly flailing about until Rose grabbed her head and pulled her out. Olive coughed, spit sand, and cried, but was all right, Rose remembered, "We never ever told our mother."

All was going well on the farm until a severe drought caused crop failure and after the cattle died, Edward moved the family to "Uncle Sam's place" south of Okreek.

Uncle Sam was the husband of Susie Butler Bordeaux, Edward's half sister. After a year, they moved to Soldier Creek near Rosebud. Later Ed became the milkman at the Rosebud boarding school, responsible for the cows on the school's farm.

Harriet's family also lived on the reservation and they kept in close touch. Her brother Ben and Edward were good friends. In March 1940, Ben was driving a truck from Mission to Rosebud when a sudden blizzard struck. After the storm, Ben was not with the truck; a search of the area did not find him. Edward did not give up and asked a medicine man to do a *Yuwipi* ceremony, meant to find lost people. Edward and his son Harvey attended, and the medicine man told them where to find the missing mam. They followed the medicine man's directions and found Ben's body on April 25, exactly where he had said it would be.

Edward's mother, Mary, built a house at Okreek where she lived with her daughters Louise and Rose Bordeaux. After the girls married and Mary died, Edward moved his family to Okreek. Rose married Paul Chekpa and inherited the property and intended to give it to her brother Ed, but never legally transferred the land. Paul Chekpa asked Ed for $200 to buy the land. He did not have it, but his daughter Jeannette paid Chekpa and the title was transferred to her. Harriet and Edward lived their lives out in that Okreek home and never paid rent to their daughter.

Okreek became a refuge for Sonny and Virginia while Jim had surgery for stomach cancer. He and Rose went to Rochester, Minnesota, for the operation and then recuperated in Sioux Falls for several weeks. Sonny was desolate, sad that his parents had to go away, but his grandpa sensed this and made a point of taking the boy with him on his many projects.

Sonny did many things with his grandpa that a city kid never got to do. In the fall, he went with his grandpa to cut the firewood and put it in the wagon pulled by a strong team of horses. They hauled the load back to the house and the next day they got more. Grandpa cut the logs into stove lengths to burn in the winter and Sonny helped stack them. They rode along the creek looking for wood, and Edward scouted for skunk holes. During the winter, the skunk hides were just right—thick and lush and Sonny helped his grandpa trap them. When Grandpa saw one, he took a long barbed wire and tangled it into the skunk's fur. Sonny's job was to pull out the skunk so that Grandpa could shoot it with his .22 rifle. Sonny became quite adept at the smelly job: "After a while the stink didn't bother me—even though it made my eyes water." On one trap run they got three skunks and Sonny happily tied them to the saddle of his horse—he was so proud of them. But their odor preceded their arrival at the house where Grandma waited as they rode into the yard. She said, "Edward, what did you do? Taking this boy and getting him all smelly?"

Grandpa said, "Well, Harriet, we was just trapping and he is proud of his skunks."

Grandpa showed Eddie how to skin them out and cure the hides. Harriet made them go to the barn, take off their clothes, and bathe. Grandma scrubbed Sonny down with soap and water and took a jar of tomato juice she had canned in the fall and poured it all over him to get rid of skunk stink. She made Grandpa promise that he would never again take the boy skunk hunting. Years later after Virginia started writing, she used this incident in her book *Jimmy Yellow Hawk*.

They also trapped muskrat and mink, which sold for good money. Ed didn't know it then, but trapping was a skill that he would use when he was older to earn some spending money.

Another time Sonny and Grandpa rode to a pasture where there was a dead horse. It stunk terribly, but they skinned it and Grandpa took the hide into Winner and sold it for five dollars, which was the same amount they got for each skunk pelt. That was the family's winter cash money. He gave Sonny twenty-five cents and the boy bought candy.

Sonny didn't have many toys to play with so Grandpa showed him how to make his own toys. He took cow joints and knuckles and made them into horses and fashioned little wire cowboys with chaps and hats—they were no more than two inches high. Sonny still has his collection of bone horses and keeps them safely wrapped. "They are precious, and I don't want to lose them," he said after showing them to Virginia seventy years later. As children they didn't know then that bone horse toys had been made from buffalo bones long before reservation days. Grandpa was carrying on a tradition.

Grandpa also taught Sonny how to make whistles. He took a stem about six inches long from a box elder tree and about as thick as his little finger. He pounded around it until the bark slid off the stem without hurting the bark. Then he cut a notch about an inch off the stem end and then split the remaining half back. He blew on it and it whistled.

Grandpa had huge hands—his fingers were big, about as big as some people's wrists and even with all the work he did milking, chopping wood, and so on, his hands were flexible enough to play the fiddle. Oh how he made that old fiddle sing. Sometimes, he'd play while Grandma played the piano and he would jig and sway while he bowed. He tried to teach Sonny how to play the Jew's harp, but the boy caught his tongue in the instrument, which pinched, and they both laughed. He showed Sonny how to cup his hands, blow into them to imitate the call of a dove. Even today, as an old man, Ed sits outside and as he blows, doves fly in from all around the yard and he remembers Grandpa Ross.

The time Sonny spent with Grandpa Ross was pleasant and took the boy's mind off missing his parent. Edward taught Sonny things that Jimmy would have, if he had been well enough to do so. Sonny and Grandpa hunted with a single shotgun, sparking what would be a lifelong passion in the boy.

They rode horses—they weren't beauties, but they were fine to ride. They rode to pastures to look for different things, like the dead horse they found. During the war when aluminum plates and rubber was in demand they rode south of Okreek into the sand hills and salvaged old rubber tires that ranchers had discarded.

Grandpa gave Sonny a horse he named Trigger because he looked Like Roy Rodger's horse. Trigger was a colt when Sonny first rode him at the gate then turned back into the fenced yard. It got so Trigger would not go any farther. Sonny's uncle Leo came home from the navy and said, "We can't have this." He rode the horse, whipped and spurred him until Trigger obeyed and Sonny could ride to the end of the road and back. After that, the horse minded so that the boy could ride with Grandpa all up and down the creek.

One time Grandpa got word that some man had shipped a load of horses on the train from Yakima, Washington, but he got stuck at the end of line at Witten and had no way to ship them farther into South Dakota. They were small horses, called Yakimas, and the owner had to dispose of them. Anybody who wanted a horse could go up there and get one. Grandpa and Sonny rode to Witten and got four horses each and led them back to Okreek. This was a great boon to the Rosses because not only did Grandpa increase his own herd from two to ten, he traded the extra horses for car batteries, team and wagon, one time for goat. He was quite skilled at barter and trade.

Looking back Sonny now understands that Grandma and Grandpa were extremely poor—as were most people on the reservation. Grandpa had a sixty-acre allotment of land east of Okreek and arranged with a farmer for a cash crop of hay and Sonny helped him cut it. But most of Grandpa's income came from trapping, seasonal haying or branding for white ranchers, and other odd jobs. He was a reliable, hard worker and was able to do about anything that was asked of him.

An old farmer out near Mission had an old collapsed barn in his pasture and said Grandpa could have the lumber if he hauled it away. It was about ten miles out, so Grandpa and Sonny took a team and wagon and worked all day stacking up the lumber and it got too late to haul it home. Rose and Jimmy were still at home then and they drove to the pasture and brought Edward and Sonny home. They drove them out next day and they hauled the lumber home. Grandpa was also a carpenter and he built an addition onto the house with that used lumber. It was a small house, about twenty feet wide and thirty feet long, and he added on a lean-to on one side to double the size of the house. After Grandpa finished the walls, the addition became Grandma's kitchen. Uncle George was going to install indoor plumbing, but that never happened. When he got the floor installed, Uncle Donald decided to have a dance. He had a windup Victrola that played records and he invited Okreek teens to come dance.

Sonny and Virginia's parents came home after Jimmy's successful surgery. Sonny was glad to be with his parents and in his home, but he missed Grandpa and visited him as often as he could as a teen and an adult.

Harriet and Edward were married almost sixty years when she died at age eighty-one of heart failure. She had always had heart problems and asthma and in her later years was often rushed to the IHS hospital in Rosebud.

On one of her frequent hospitalizations, she was certain she was dying. "Edward," she said to her husband of fifty years, "what will you do after I am gone?"

Edward patted her hand and thought a minute. "Well, your bridesmaid is still alive." That time, Grandma got well.

After Grandma's death, Grandpa insisted on living alone in the house they had shared. Years later, when Sonny returned to the reservation, he helped the old man as much as he could, but he was an independent old cuss and didn't want any help. He was working on his old car when somehow it rolled over his leg and broke it. He struggled into the car and drove himself to the IHS hospital in Rosebud where his leg was set and a cast applied. His daughters, aunts Dolly and Olive, had jobs and couldn't take care of him, so Sonny took him to live at Ring Thunder.

Sonny set up one of the tribal houses for Grandpa near the ranch house nearby and he seemed content to be there. He liked to sit out in the sun and watch others working on the ranch.

"One day," Ed recalled, "Carmen came home with about a dozen chickens and she and Ray tried to ring their necks then chop off their heads. They didn't do too well and yelled and hollered as the chickens hopped around with heads half off, spraying blood all over Carmen and the kids. Grandpa laughed so hard, he about fell off of his chair."

Another time the youngest boy, Leo, was alone with the old man and Grandpa asked for a screwdriver and then used it to chip his cast to pieces until it fell off. Somehow his leg healed anyway, but his daughters decided that he should go to the nursing home in Valentine because he needed more help than they could give him. Sonny didn't want him to go, but had no say in the decision. Besides, it was a lot of work for Carmen.

Eddie remembered, "Grandpa didn't complain about Valentine and we all visited him as often as we could. Carmen and cousin Alma went over one day and smuggled in a pint of whiskey to him. They didn't know that Virginia and Vance had been there and brought him a bottle too. Grandpa drank it all at once and got a bit rowdy—singing and trying to dance. The head of the home scolded Alma and Carmen and told them not to do that anymore.

"He liked to sit outdoors whenever he could, and no one bothered him. One day he fell and couldn't get up. He crawled all around the building to the front door before somebody saw him and helped him into the building."

All the residents ate together in the dining room. "Grandpa sat next to a guy that shouted for no reason. Grandpa told him 'Shut Up!' but the man kept hollering. Grandpa took his cane and put it in the man's mouth, 'That'll shut him up!' he said even though the aides scolded him."

He died at Valentine on May 17, 1983. He was a special person to Sonny and Virginia, who wrote a poem that summed up Grandpa's life.

Grandpa Was a Cowboy and an Indian

Grandpa was a cowboy and an Indian
And he would often be confused,
'Cause he didn't look like either one,

A fact he often mused.
His pa was a white freighter
Who drove mule-pulled wagon trains.
His ma, a Lakota maid,
A nomad of the plains.

Grandpa did a fancy jig
while his fiddle played along,
Or he'd croon the long, sad verses
To old-time cowboy songs.
Still, he sang Lakota chants
Of proud lost warrior days,
Stepped high in bells and moccasins
To the beat of Indian ways.

Grandpa wrangled for white ranchers
From the Keyapaha to the Jim,
'Til he wed a Santee maiden
Then on his allotment, his own spread did begin.
Grandpa raised hoses and cattle
That thrived on prairie grass.
'Til the ranch died with the cattle
And the *Keyapaha* ceased to flow.

Grandpa was still an Indian
When his cowboy days were done,
Then he rode the range of memories
Of ways forever gone.
Tiyospaye mourned his passing
And the drum beat at his wake,
While gospel hymns were harmonized,
Beseeching God his soul to take.

Grandpa's a cowboy and an Indian
In God's eternal band
Where he'll ride forever
In heaven's prairie land.

Grandpa was buried by Harriet in the Okreek cemetery. His cowboy hat lay on his chest and an eagle feather was in his hand; a drum slowly beat as singers chanted a warrior's farewell.

Both Sonny and Virginia have fond memories of being with their grandparents in Okreek, especially after, as Sonny remembered it, how "things started to go sour" because his father was wretchedly and painfully ill with cancer. He went Sioux Falls for surgery and part of his stomach was removed. When he came home, he had no energy to do anything and was in lot of pain. But he slowly recovered, felt better, and gained weight—he looked good and it was a great time of life again. They went fishing at the dams, picked wild cherries and plums, and went pheasant hunting. The men in Okreek saved up money to get shells for the single-shell shotguns—only three in the whole community. Rose drove the car, the shooters riding on the fenders, and drove over two-track country roads; the pheasants flushed, and the men shot. They had a whole trunk load of pheasants to take home. They dressed them and then had a community feed. One time they got a big jackrabbit and ate it with the birds.

Donald and Dolly, Rose's youngest brother and sister, were teenagers at that time and Dolly had a boyfriend, Jim Haukass. Ed recalled, "Every evening those teens would gather up at the store, which was about mile from Grandma's house. Boys and girls paired up to walk, smooch, and such. Grandma told Dolly, 'You have to take Sonny with you to keep an eye on you.' So, I followed them, but they gave me a nickel and I'd forget about where they were until just about dark when they came to get me and we walked back home and I'd be a nickel richer."

Sonny came home one evening with a fever and said he hurt all over and his parents feared that he might have polio. They called Mr. Miller from the school and the BIA representative in Okreek. He checked Sonny out and told the folks to watch him—it might indeed be polio. They were at the Ross house and Sonny was very ill, his legs and back hurt when he moved, and all were afraid that he might become paralyzed. He lay there for two days, and then on the third he felt better, got up, and was fine. There was no explanation for the frightening episode, but it was worrisome during the time the nation was experiencing a polio epidemic.

Sonny, who was now called Eddie, was a mischievous kid, but usually the folks only scolded him and never spanked him. "But one time I really got in trouble," Eddie remembered. "My buddy Farrell and I snuck out at night and slept in a haystack. We never thought about our parents being worried, but they had a search team going up and down the creek, hoping we hadn't fallen in and drowned. We were seven and eight years old and, in the morning, came casually strolling up to the house. Oh, Dad was mad! 'Don't you know we had the whole place looking for you—thought you were hurt!' He pulled off his belt, but Mom and Grandma Ross and Grandma Driving Hawk followed him, 'Don't hit him!' they yelled. I ran through the house—living room, to the kitchen, into the back bedrooms, back to the living room and he was right after me swinging that belt. But I was too fast and he didn't get me. When he got too close, I dove under my bed and slid way back where he couldn't reach me. He grabbed me by one leg and Mom had him by one leg and the grandmas were pulling at his arms. 'Don't hit him! Don't hit him!' I cried and yelled as loud as I could and finally he let me go.

"I had never seen him so angry and I don't know if he would have used the belt or not, I know he really was upset and worried about me." Beside that one time, "I don't remember him ever hitting me and neither did Mom."

James had Sunday services in Okreek and then he'd drive out to small reservation chapels at Ideal and Witten. After Virginia learned to play the organ, she went with him to play for hymn singing. Her legs were too short to work the pumps to get the sound, and so James had blocks of wood tied to her shoes so that she could pump and play. During the fall, she learned to drive on the trips over country roads. She drove slowly in low gear while Jimmy kept his gun ready to shoot a pheasant.

The Ideal community was about fifteen miles north of Winner where Jimmy went once a month, and because there was no priest at the white church in Winner, he filled in there as well. A white rancher north of Winner had a daughter who wanted to be married and he asked James to do the wedding service. The fact that James was Indian upset all the rednecks in Winner who didn't think he should marry a white couple. That didn't bother the rancher though, and the ceremony was on the ranch with a big feed and dance—it was gay old time—anyway, that was a way to overcome the prejudice in Winner.

Rose was dark haired but fair skinned and didn't look Indian so she had no problem shopping in Winner, but when it came time to service their car, the white mechanics wouldn't wait on Jimmy, so Rose took the car in.

That was discrimination, but the children did not realize it at the time. They went to Winner with Grandma and Grandpa Driving Hawk to shop for groceries. The Outlaw Trading Post was a store that had everything, and Indians were not banned from shopping there. Still they could not all go in at once so Grandma sat outside with other Indian women and they gossiped with all their friends. One by one, they would go into store to shop after another came out. There were other stores on Main Street, but Indians were not welcomed there, so most of them shopped at the Outlaw store.

The family enjoyed the Labor Day celebration in Winner and had fun on the carnival rides, but the only place the Indians could use the restrooms was at the courthouse. There were guards who would let a person go downstairs to use the bathroom. The only other place was the park, which Sonny liked better than the courthouse, which felt like going into a dungeon.

Eddie did not know there was also discrimination in Okreek. The Indian children attended a government day school, but across the creek was the public school, where the white kids went. They accepted that and didn't think much about it. Then later when Eddie went to Todd County High School in Mission, the Indian boys had to take their lunch and eat in the study hall. Across the street were Quonsets where the white kids ate, and they had a dorm where they stayed.

Many kids had small portion of Indian blood but didn't want to be Indian and wouldn't eat with them. One was Charlie Colome, who was one-sixteenth Indian, but back then he claimed he was all white and stayed in the white dormitory and ate in the white Quonset.

When Sonny moved back in the seventies and went to a tribal council meeting, there sat Charlie Colome. Sonny said, "Oh boy, do they let white people in council meetings now?" They said no, it was only Indians. It was confusing—a person claimed Indian blood when it benefitted him.

Again James was ill and had to go to Sioux Falls for treatment, Sonny stayed in Springfield, South Dakota, with Grandma and Grandpa Driving Hawk. Grandpa was employed as the janitor for Saint Mary's school for Indian girls and Grandma was the laundress. The students called them "Mr. and Mrs. DH" and really appreciated them because they were able to offer comfort to homesick little girls and to encourage their efforts in school.

Grandpa Robert Driving Hawk was from the Lower Brule Reservation in South Dakota. He was raised by an aunt after his parents died of smallpox. He attended the Indian school at Chamberlain where Grandma Flora was also a student. The students were separated according to gender wherever they were on the campus. Boys' dorms and girls' dorm; they ate at separate tables and there was a wide aisle between desks in the classroom. Still the boys and girls managed to get together. Some sixty years later Grandma told how she and Robert courted.

"My girlfriend said that her brother said that Robert wanted to see me that evening. Even though we weren't supposed to be out at night, kids did sneak out. I took my blanket and went out. Robert came, and we wrapped the blanket around us and he gave me an apple. We weren't doing anything—just standing close, but we got caught. Robert was expelled—he went back to Lower Brule. I stayed, but had only bread and water to eat. I felt bad and thought I'd never see him again. When I went home, my dad scolded me for shaming him with this boy. It was a bad time, because he had a new wife after my mother died and she didn't like me. But then Robert came."

Robert had caught a ride on the mail wagon from Chamberlain all 122 miles to Rosebud, then walked the four miles to the Ring Thunder community where Flora lived.

"We walked to Rosebud to the Episcopal church and got married. Then we got a ride to Valentine in Nebraska. We got on the train and there were Indians from Pine Ridge going all the way to New York, then they'd get on a boat to England. They were with Buffalo Bill's show.

"My aunt was there and said, 'Are you running away with this man?'

"'No,' I told her and showed her our wedding license. Then she gave me a big piece of *wasna* [a dried mix of buffalo or beef with choke cherries] for a wedding present.

"We got off at Sioux City and went to a hotel."

This was Flora's first time in a white town and she was frightened. "I made Robert sit up all night in front of the door—guarding me." Tears came as she remembered, "Poor thing. It was his wedding night."

The train took them from Sioux City to Chamberlain on the west side of the Missouri River, where Robert's uncle waited for them. They rode to Lower Brule and to the small cabin Robert had built for them. But they stayed there only a few years. When Flora heard her father was dying they moved to Rosebud. They lived on her allotment in the Ring Thunder area and had four children, but James was the only one to live to adulthood. Paul and Elizabeth died as babies; David was a victim of the influenza epidemic that swept through the reservation in 1920. Then Margaret died of diphtheria in Grandpa's arms. James was their only surviving child. They moved to the town of Mission where Robert worked at the Phillips 66 station and both were active in Trinity Episcopal church for many years until they were offered jobs at Saint Mary's in Springfield.

Springfield, so named after the many springs in the area, sat on the bluffs of the Missouri, on a point of land overlooking the Missouri River. Across the river was Santee, Nebraska, home of the Santee Dakota who were exiled there after the 1862 Minnesota uprising. Reservation Indians once poled bullboats across and in the winter traversed the ice to visit relatives on either side. Saint Mary's was located at the town's edge near the bluffs overlooking the river. It was a large two-story sandstone building with a large green expanse in front and a laundry building, shop, and vegetable garden on the side. Robert Driving Hawk was the janitor who cared for the grounds and Flora was in charge of laundering the students' and staff's clothing and linens. When their parents traveled to Rochester, Minnesota, for Jimmy's surgery and treatment, Virginia was a student at the school while Sonny lived with his grandparents in a house on the school's campus.

Eddie found it strange living in a white community where there were only two Indians in elementary school. The Drapeaus, a Yankton Indian family, lived in Springfield and there was a boy in Eddie's class, but they had an older son, Dick Drapeau, who was a big teen hero in high school sports. When he graduated, he went on to Southern State Teachers College, also in Springfield, where he played football. Later, Dick became a BIA worker and Eddie met him several times at the Aberdeen BIA area office.

Eddie did well in school and fit in well. When he was nine years old there was a notice at the school asking boxing students to enter matches at the legion hall. Always the adventurer, Eddie asked his grandparents if he could enter the tournament. Grandma was opposed to it, but Grandpa gave him the fifty cents entry fee. He thought it was strange that Grandpa didn't go in the gym to watch the match but stood outside and watched Eddie through the door. As an adult Eddie realized that Grandpa was not welcome in the hall. He was thrilled that the boy won in his age group and proudly clapped while Eddie was awarded a small trophy. They walked home, Eddie excitedly reliving the match and happily showing his prize to Grandma, who said, "I suppose you think you're Joe Louis now."

Every evening after school Eddie helped Grandpa with the janitorial chores. In the winter he carried a five-pound can of ashes from the girls' dorm furnace and dumped it on the driveway for added traction. In the summer he helped mow the lawn, which seemed to be an endless job, walking back and forth an enormous lawn at the school, but he appreciated the twenty-five cents a week that he earned.

Every evening before bed, Grandma's insisted that the boy read the Bible. "I read it and read it," Eddie recalled, "but I didn't understand it with all the 'Thees and Thous' in it but I read it every night."

Jimmy's condition worsened and he went back to Rochester where he learned there was nothing more that could be done for him. He was admitted to the Yankton Hospital where he died.

2

A Kid in Uniform

"DAD DIED," ED QUIETLY REMEMBERED THE AGONIZ-
ingly painful loss to the boy who had adored his father. James
was too young when he died of stomach cancer on May 22,
1948—only thirty-four years old; Rose was thirty-three, Virginia
fourteen, and Eddie twelve. They buried James in the Trinity
Episcopal Cemetery in Mission in the lot where Grandpa Driving Hawk joined him in 1957 and Grandma in 1977. His death
devastated the old couple—Grandpa said he should have died
first; James was their only child who had lived to adulthood. At
the funeral, Robert and Flora clung together and wept. Eddie
was on crutches because of a knee injured in a ball game—
that made it even tougher for him to get through the service
at the graveside: "I couldn't raise my hand to wipe my eyes or
blow my nose."

Not only did Rose and the children grieve James's loss, they
were now poor and homeless.

Before James's final illness, the Driving Hawks had lived in
Greenwood, South Dakota, where he was the priest in charge
of the Episcopal missions on the Yankton Reservation. The
church and rectory were in Greenwood, a small village in a
fertile green area near the Missouri River where Sonny and
his buddies caught gar and catfish.

The large white church had been the cathedral of Bishop
Hobart Hare, Dakota Territories' first Episcopal bishop. The
nearby rectory, painted like the church building, was a wonderful home for the Driving Hawks. No longer did Rose have

to heat water for baths in a tin tub; there was a bathroom with a porcelain tub and toilet. Sonny did not have to haul water from an outdoor well and they could easily read by the electric lights, and to Rose the most wonderful thing was an electric refrigerator in the kitchen.

After James's death Rose and the children had to vacate the rectory. Rose's brothers George and Harvey came from Sioux Falls and Flandreau to move them to Okreek to live with Grandma and Grandpa Ross. That summer, Rose got a job as a cook for the employees at the BIA Agency in Rosebud and Virginia helped her. They stayed in the small apartment at the employees' housing complex. Eddie again stayed with the Rosses. The little family was torn apart and never again did they live together for any length of time.

In the fall, Rose and Virginia moved back to Springfield, where Rose was dorm mother at Saint Mary's school, an Episcopal boarding school for Indian girls, and where Virginia was a student. Eddie stayed in Mission and attended the public school while living at Hare School, a boarding home for Indian boys. It was a large two-story white frame building with dormitories on the top floor, kitchen and dining rooms on the first floor, as well as a large common room for the boys' study and recreation time. On the campus were two houses for the school's staff, a barn for the milk cows, and a stone chapel that later was named "The James Driving Hawk Chapel," for James had also been a Hare School boy.

While working at Saint Mary's, Rose took classes at Southern State Teachers College in Springfield and earned an associate of arts degree in secretarial science. Rose was hired by the Episcopal Diocese as the bishop's secretary and the family moved to Sioux Falls.

Virginia graduated from Saint Mary's and enrolled at South Dakota State College in Brookings. Eddie attended Washington High School and made the varsity teams and lettered in football, basketball, and track, for a total of nine letters. Still,

A Kid in Uniform

he never felt a part of the school since he was a new kid and most of the others had grown up together. He played quarterback for the second-string team and in one game he recovered six fumbles; in another, he caught a pass and ran for a touchdown. He ran in an in-state track tournament and took second in the open half mile. He enjoyed sports, but the racist comments of opposing teams annoyed him. "Hey buck" or "wahoo," with fake hooting war calls and intentionally rough body slams, got to him. That summer of 1952 he didn't have much to do so he asked Rose if he could go back to Mission and Hare School for a summer job. He also had another reason for moving back: the year before he had met Carmen Boyd, and he wanted to see more of her.

Mr. John Artichoker was the headmaster of Hare School; his wife, Emily, was the housemother and cook. The boys called them "Mr. and Mrs. A." Mr. A. had been an athlete and coach and trained the boys as if they were prepping for a big game. Every day after school, they ran a mile and then a mile back. Eddie thought about his father, who had believed his daily runs cured his tuberculosis. He was diagnosed in his teens and IHS wanted to send him to Rapid City's Sioux Sanitorium, the TB treatment center for Indians in North and South Dakota. After the tribes were moved to reservations, TB was rampant among families crowded together in small houses— not much more than shacks—which were rarely cleaned. In the old days, when a tepee was soiled, it was moved to a new location. It was only after girls went to boarding schools that they learned about cleanliness and sanitation.

James's parents didn't want him to go to Sioux San because it had a history of youngsters dying there, and their bodies were buried in the sanitorium's cemetery, far away from home. They went to see Father Barbour and asked him what to do. Fortunately, Father Barbour knew how TB was treated back east where he had lived in Connecticut. A regime of fresh air, healthy diet, and exercise was the treatment. The story was that Jimmy ran every day and he was cured. Now, Eddie ran to keep myself in shape.

Father Barbour, James's friend and mentor, kept an eye on Eddie and the other boys living at Hare School for the summer. Farrell Dillion, an Okreek buddy, and Eddie earned seven dollars a week milking two cows every morning and night, used the separator for cream, and after it was sold, they got to keep the milk check. They also painted the old main building and kept the basement, showers, and barn clean. Ted Rouillard, one of Eddie's best friends, liked the duty of cleaning the church basement, sweeping the floor and checking the hot water heater, because he could smoke down there and not get caught.

They nailed a tin can at the end of the long walls and the basement became a court for "tin can ball," where they dunked tennis balls. Eddie like being with his friends who were as mischievous as he was. Ed recalled, "Mr. A. kept strict control of the school—we knew this but liked to tease him. When we were on the second floor we rolled marbles across the wooden floor. Down below they sounded like cannons booming. Soon we'd hear Mr. A. tromping heavily up the stairs. Of course, when he got up to our dorm, we were all quiet in bed.

"Teddy did a real good impression of the way Mr. A. walked—heavy step and swinging arms. He'd walk behind Mr. A. and we had a hard time not laughing, but he was caught when Mr. A. turned around to see what was so funny."

Near the school campus was a small pond made by the damming of Antelope Creek where they boys swam. There Eddie, with Teddy's help, used the skill he'd learned from Grandpa Ross to trap beaver and muskrats in the stream. They sold the pelts for sixty-five dollars and were the richest boys at school. Eddie was glad to make his own money because his mother was unable to send him much spending money.

The summer when Ed went to Hare School rather than staying in Sioux Falls, he recalled, "There wasn't much to do in the evenings at Hare School. One boring evening I decided to treat Farrell to a game in the pool hall in Mission. Mr. and Mrs. Artichoker were gone and left Father Ned Moore, a new young priest for the Rosebud Mission, in charge. He followed us into the pool hall and ordered, 'You boys get out of this den of iniquity, this sinful place! Plus, you left the campus without permission!'"

The boys protested, they didn't know they had to have permission and resented the priest assuming they were doing something evil. But he didn't listen and ordered them back to the school, "You boys are restricted to the campus until school starts." The boys thought the priest unfair—not even giving them a chance to explain—and told him to "go to hell," which further antagonized the man.

Eddie and Farrell fumed all night then the next morning they went to see Father Barbour and told him what had happened with Father Moore. Father Barbour tried to reason with them, that it was only a few weeks before school started and that they should stay, but the boys were adamant about leaving and asked for their money earned painting the building. He gave them forty dollars each and they left. They hitched a ride to Okreek, and Eddie went to Grandma and Grandpa Ross's place. Father Barbour called Rose and she and Virginia came to take Eddie back to Sioux Falls, he was determined not to go back to Hare School. Nor did he want to go back to Washington High School and wasn't sure what to do. His mother and grandparents could not persuade him otherwise.

Back in Sioux Falls, Eddie found a job helping a farmer harvest grain, but he was restless and unhappy. Then friend Ted Roulliard came by and said he was enlisting in the army. Eddie decided that's what he wanted to do. Rose consulted with her brother George, a World War II veteran, who advised her to let the boy do it: "It'll make a man of him." Rose reluctantly agreed, and wished Jimmy were there to help with their son. She worried about the boy going to war in Korea.

She went with Eddie to the marine, army, and navy recruiting offices, but they all had a three-month waiting period. However, the air force recruiter said, "I'll take you tomorrow, but you have to pass a test." Eddie easily passed the test, and Rose signed the papers giving her permission for the seventeen-year-old to enlist. "On the twenty-ninth of August, 1952," Eddie recalled, "I belonged to the United States Air Force."

Rose and Virginia took him to the bus depot and saw him off with only a toothbrush and they wept to see him go—he was so young. The bus took him to San Antonio, Texas, where he transferred to another bus that took him to the basic training site at Lackland Air Force Base. The base in Bexar County, Texas, was and is the only entry processing station for air force basic training.

Eddie recalled, "I did not have much problem with basic training as I had been living in a dormitory at Hare School and was used to getting up early in the morning. It didn't bother me to sleep in a room with other guys and I knew how to make my bed—it wasn't much different in the air force. I learned how to march, shine my shoes, and learn all the military orders and restrictions that I would live by. I had a crew cut when I got there so it did not bother me to have more cut off. Some of the other recruits from Chicago had ducktails and cried to have their hair cut. I went through basic training and got along good with the other men and the TI [training instructor]. I had no problems with the tough physical drills and calisthenics because I was in good athletic form and could run faster than the other guys in the platoon."

Always ready to try something new, Eddie joined the base's boxing team and in addition to the regular physical drills, he practiced in the ring. "It was fun sparring with other boxers but then I entered a tournament. I fought three fights and lost three fights. I figured I wasn't cut out to be a boxer even though I liked to hear the crowd cheer when I got in the ring, but it wasn't too thrilling to get beat up." Eddie gave up boxing.

A Kid in Uniform

But because he was an athlete and on the boxing team during basic training, he didn't have any other grueling details because an athlete's main job was training. His sunny personality led him to enjoy his fellow airmen and even basic training wasn't hard save for the Texas temperatures. "Working out in the heat—doing the pull-ups, push-ups in ninety-five-degree weather was tough. It was so hot we did not march and stayed in the barracks and shined shoes. Whenever it got below ninety-five, we fell out no matter what time of the day—even in the middle of the night—and marched. Half of the day we marched and the other half we spent in the classroom learning suitable things useful to a young seventeen-year-old boy. I never had social studies or hygiene in school, so I studied that and learned how to live with a bunch of guys, how to salute and behave in an acceptable military manner."

There was an impressive graduation ceremony at the end of basic training. All the graduating flights fell out on the fields marching to the bands playing patriotic tunes and they formed up and stood at ease to listen to speeches urging them to be proud and diligent airmen. "The ceremony made me proud about completing basic training," Ed recalled. Many parents attended the graduation, but they lived nearby. "I wished Mom were there, but I knew she could not afford the long trip from Sioux Falls."

He had earned seventy-five dollars a month upon enlistment and after basic training now made a hundred a month, from which twelve dollars was deducted for war bonds, which he sent to Rose. "I really did not need much money anyway—my bed and meals were provided and the little cash I had was for cigarettes or snacks. After basic we got free alcohol at the airmen's club and I enjoyed the drinks and even though I got falling-down drunk, sick, threw up, and had terrible hangovers," he and the other young men would do it again and again.

After graduation, the trainees took aptitude tests as a guide to what their duties in the air force would be. Eddie's determined that he would be a good butcher and cook, which surprised him a bit. "I guess I learned to butcher with Grandpa Ross when we skinned critters, but I had never cooked anything, and I sure didn't want to do it in the service." He looked at the other training options and decided to get into air traffic control and was pleased when his next assignment was Keesler AFB in Biloxi, Mississippi. Keesler was the air force's air education and training base and its mission was training airmen for active duty. Thirty-five men were assigned to the traffic control course and on a hot October day they flew to Biloxi. Texas had been hot, and Mississippi was too, but the high humidity made it seem hotter. After checking into their barracks, they then were told that thirty-five men was not enough for a class.

"We waited two more weeks for more men to show up so that the course could be offered. It was a dull time with no duties other than lie around the barracks until we were ordered to pick up rocks and sometimes get in trouble for not picking up the right rocks. Our master sergeant had a scam going. He told us that we wouldn't have to do KP duty if we gave him some cash. We didn't because we were so bored that doing KP didn't bother us, but I hated washing pots and pans. Some of us figured how to get out of it—we crawled up into the space above the cupboards and hid there for an hour until the shift ended. The cook didn't know who we were and couldn't report us.

"Finally, they told us that there was not enough for the class, and we had to take a radar operator course instead." The thirty-five men learned to read radar, how to talk to the airplanes, put a Tipsy 1B radar set together—a small unit that came in four different pieces plus the battery transmitter and antennae receiver. They graduated from that class and were sent to a forward observer course where they learned to direct aircraft over a battlefield. "We learned how to send messages in Morse code and to receive them. We were supposed to be able to transmit at twenty words per minute, but I'd never taken a typing class, and my fingers wouldn't move that fast, but I was able to write that fast with a pencil." Nevertheless, he finally passed the course and completed the Radar and Radio Operator course, Aircraft Control Operator course, and Water and Jungle Survival course.

At Keesler, Ed, along with other young airmen in his group, started heavy drinking when off duty. It was part of becoming a man; they all did it and no superior officer tried to temper the boozing if it didn't interfere with their duties.

"After we finished the course, there was another big graduation ceremony, right after Christmas. We were told that if we volunteered for the Forward Observer course, we could choose the place we wanted to go for an overseas assignment. We picked Switzerland, England, or other nice European places. We big dummies believed them and volunteered. After the graduation ceremony, it started raining so we waited in the barracks for the duty postings on the outdoor bulletin board. When we spotted the sergeant tacking up a list, we ran to look, then raced back in when we saw it wasn't ours. Finally, our assignments were posted and none of us got places we wanted; we were all going to Korea.

"I had thirty-day leave before we had to report to Omaha, Nebraska, to sign in and from there to Camp Stoneman, California." Ed rode a bus to Sioux Falls with a stop at Jackson, Mississippi, where he spent two days with a buddy then went on. "I stayed with Mom in Sioux Falls for a couple weeks. I wanted to go to Mission to see Carmen, who knew I was coming because we wrote letters as often as we could."

Rose worked as the Episcopal bishops' secretary and her brother George gave her an old Chrysler he had fixed so she could drive about town. Ed asked his uncle if the car could make it to Mission and back. George told him he thought it would, but that it used oil, but he had to take extra oil on hand and keep an eye on the gauge. "I headed to Mission and right away found that the car burned oil so fast that I had to fill up about every fifty miles and the trip took a long while." When he got to Mission, he leaned that Carmen was still at Saint Francis Indian Mission School, so he drove on to Rosebud where he stopped at Rose's sister Olive's and her husband Ralph's in Rosebud. Olive had served as a WAAC in World War II and sympathized with her nephew's desire to see his girl before going to war. He told them about the car using oil, so they kindly let him use their car to go to Saint Francis.

The mission and the small town around it, named after Saint Francis Assisi, was founded in 1886 and was once known as "where the Black Robes live," referring to the color of the long black garment the Jesuits wore. The missionary Brothers spoke German and during World War I, were suspected of espionage. A story went around the reservation that there was a radio transmitter in the church's bell tower on which American secrets were sent to Germany. Untrue, of course, for what kind of military intelligence reached the middle of the reservation? But it was a good story.

At the time Carmen attended, the mission ran a boarding school for boys and girls on the reservation and taught academic and Catholic tenets. It was known for its rigorous discipline and the comingling of sexes was prohibited. So, Ed was not surprised when he was sent to a big hall about half the size of a basketball court and a nun came, asked him what he wanted. "I'd like to see Carmen Boyd." The Sister responded, "Only family can visit students."

"Please?" Ed asked. "I'm going to Korea."

The nun looked at him a while and then said, "We will make an exception this time since you are in uniform." She went to get Carmen.

Ed waited alone in the empty hall for what seemed like hours but was only fifteen minutes. Finally, Carmen came, following the nun who made her sit about two chairs away from Ed, and the nun sat next to the girl. "We talked for an hour and then the nun told me to leave," Ed recalled. "She let us have one little old kiss before I left for Korea."

Ed drove back to Rosebud and then took the old Chrysler to Okreek. Grandma and Grandpa Ross were delighted to see him and his old dog Fritz, one of Soup's pups—about fifteen years old. Grandpa looked over the Chrysler and shook his head. "Hope you make it back to Sioux Falls." Harriet had good corn soup and fry bread for supper, which Ed relished. He was happily at home with his grandparents. The next morning, he tried to be cheerful when he said goodbye, but choked up when Grandma wiped her eyes and Grandpa shook his hand.

Numbly he drove back to Sioux Falls with many stops to replace the oil the old car burned (plus somehow it now had a cracked window). Back at Rose's, Uncle George came and said the car's engine needed repair and it needed a new window. Ed said, "I can pay for it," but George said he would do it. As a WWII veteran who had seen duty in the Pacific, he knew what it was like to go to war.

Rose and Virginia saw Ed off on a bus to Omaha, Nebraska, and again wept at his going—even though he had grown taller and filled out more as a man in uniform, he was still so young and would be going to a dangerous place. In Omaha he reported to the army at the train depot where an officer signed off on his leave, and he boarded a troop train filled with navy, army, and air force men going to Korea. Most of them were draftees and they were not at all happy about being called up. He found two buddies he knew from the Forward Observer course and they joked, played cards, and had a good time. After the train ride, they rode a bus to Camp Stoneman in Pittsburg, California, received their barrack and number assignment, and were told to jump when they heard their number called, ready for the next duty.

"While we waited at Camp Stoneman for our next assignment, we had KP duty—washing pots and pans, but we just walked out of the kitchen—just like at Kessler—the cook didn't know who we were and couldn't report us."

They were restricted to base, but the three mischievous

teenagers crawled under the fence, got to town, and hit the bars. They bought six bottles of cheap whiskey and got a cab back to base, whose the driver suggested, "Why don't you put your bottles in the trunk, so that when we're stopped before you enter the base, they'll search you, but not the trunk," Ed remembered with a wry smile at his young gullibility. "So, we did—we got out and the guards patted us down and the cab drove off with our booze. That was only one of the of the crazy things I did—a teenage kid out on his own with no restrictions on drinking."

Finally, D14, Ed's number, was called, and he went over to a big tent for processing to go to Korea. "We took off all our clothes and were examined from head to foot. Medics stood on each side of the line and gave us injections—six shots—three in each arm. One man ahead of me turned pale and fainted—he was not too crazy about getting shots. They moved him to the side, and we kept moving. We got dressed, picked up our duffel bags, and lined up for about a mile on the side of a hill and slowly made our way down to a ferry to take us out to the ships.

"I was a seventeen-year-old kid in a man's uniform, but I didn't admit to others that I was worried about what was going to happen. It was all so new and strange and different than being on the reservation and I was scared yet excited about what would happen." On February 26, 1953, they boarded a ferry to the USS *Mann* that transported three thousand men. "At the dock the troops were given a big send off as the crowd cheered and a band played to make us feel patriotic about our duty. The Salvation Army gave us free coffee and doughnuts, which was great. For all the time I was in the service ten cents was deducted from my pay for the Red Cross, who charged us for coffee and doughnuts.

"We got green or pink cards that determined our deck assignment on the ship. The ferry moved slow, but men were already getting seasick and throwing up." Ed felt nauseous at the sight and smell of others' vomit but did not get sick. "On the ship, our sleeping spots were six bunks high on the bottom deck and I had the third tier of the bed, and there was just barely room to slide in and out. A big man sagged down above so that I couldn't turn over. It was awful! All around me men were puking, moaning and groaning, and floor was slick with vomit—it was an awful stink and even though it was hosed down every morning it was a mess. I got out of there, took my new issued blanket and overcoat and moved to the top deck. It was heck of a lot better than down in the hole and I spent two days up there.

"Movies were shown on the quarter deck, but good seats were tough to get. My buddies and I hung over the rail and pretended to gag like we were going to throw up. The guys below us left their seats rather than have us vomit on them, then we ran to get their seats.

"We were fifteen days on the ship, and I enjoyed the experience. I learned a lot about life at sea, but also about gambling. When I was growing up at Okreek, Willie Wright, Grandpa Ross's half brother, visited occasionally, and he taught me how to play dice with other teen boys. When I won, I put the cash in a tin can and buried it down by the corner of road to Grandpa's yard. When I went up to the store, I'd stop, get some money for what I wanted, and no one ever found it. Now, on the ship, I thought I knew how to shoot craps, but, when I played with black troops, they had a whole different way of playing and even had their own language, but I learned how to play their way and before the trip was over I won quite a bit of money.

"While was at Camp Stoneman I bought *I, the Jury* by Mickey Spillane, which was the closest thing to pornography I had ever encountered, and others wanted to read it, so I rented it for fifty cents a day. Whenever I got fifty cents, I'd shoot dice. I kept that book going all the way to Korea and it paid every day."

The ship docked in Honolulu, Hawaii, and the men had shore leave and headed to the bars. In one, there was a tank of goldfish and the young drunks thought it was fun to scoop up a fish and swallow it whole. They drank until they could barely see and were thoroughly soused and disorderly so that the shore patrol arrested them and threw them in the ship's brig. Then the air police ordered them down to their bunks to stay there. Hawaii was hot, muggy, and miserable, but the heat was worse in the bunks down in the hole. All were severely hungover the next day.

After eleven days, the ship docked at Yokohama, Japan, but the Eight Air Force Forward Observers were the last ones to unload. They landed at six in the morning, stood on deck all day, and watched everybody else march off until they were called at nine o'clock that night. All were famished, they had not eaten all day, but they were loaded on a bus and driven to Johnson Air Force Base. Then they boarded a c-47 plane, flew to Korea, and went directly to k16, which was Kesan, Korea, on the west coast, about twenty miles south of the thirty-eighth parallel. Ed had turned eighteen on March 1, on the ship, and now it was March 10 when they landed at midnight.

Sergeant Pina, a man of Italian heritage, took charge of the men as they got off the bus. He was a former World War II tank commander and was bitter to be called to active duty again. He had been in the Army National Guard and when he found out they might go to Korea he transferred to the Air National Guard but ended up in Korea anyway. "He reminded me of a buffalo because of his barrel chest and he bellowed like one when he yelled at the new boots—us airmen first class. It was like being in basic again. He marched us to a sixteen-man tent, our new home where he also slept. He kept us in line at base, but never went on any missions with us. We dumped our duffel bags and finally got to march to the mess tent for midnight chow. It was delicious even though it was only powdered eggs and creamed beef on toast. I loved it with a little sausage in it and catsup. I thought it was tasty. The creamed beef, called sos, shit on a shingle, was a little chalky, but I was eighteen years old, hungry all the time, and I wolfed it down.

"That meal was not at all like the first meal I had in basic training. When I got off the bus a Lackland AFB, I marched to the mess hall and was served a big steak, baked potato, and corn on the cob. I had never had such a meal while growing up in Okreek or at Hare School and thought 'Boy, they really feed good in the air force.' However, that was the last meal I ever had like that over the twenty years I was in the service."

Nine men made up the forward observer crews on duty in Korea and a marine was assigned to give them cover if needed. Lieutenant Valentine was the control officer who assigned four men a 30-caliber machine gun to take up the hill; Ed toted the barrel, the lightest part, and others carried the rest. They rode in a jeep to the assigned mission and set up the TPS 1B radar mobile system and waited for the B29s to fly. They contacted the bombers and directed them to the site where the bombs were dropped.

Ed found it an exhilarating experience for a young kid who did not know any better. His crew guided the bombers in and watched the explosions about twenty to thirty miles away. They carried out many similar missions or sometimes directed fighter aircraft to where the army was being attacked. After a mission, they went back to K16 and lay off for a couple of days and answered to Sarge Pina for everything they did—he kept them strictly in line.

Ed's last mission in Korea was May 12, 1953, when his unit set up the radar to bring in B29s. "It was about two in the afternoon when we rode a jeep as far up as it could go and then walked to the top of the mountain to set up the operation; the marines were running cover as usual but it looked to me like they were napping while we set up. Anyway, we were caught unawares, and all hell busted loose! The Chinese came running and shooting and everybody was firing. The lieutenant blew up our radar system and told us to get down the hill as fast as we could. I took off running with everybody else scrambling as fast as we could. I felt a hard-stiff punch in my leg, fell, and rolled about halfway down the hill. I got up and ran on to the bottom of the hill where the army and navy corpsmen unit was. I ran with half of the flesh flopping from my leg from my shredded pants. I was directed to the navy unit tent and all the while cannons were shooting and booming up there on the hill. I was excited, but also terrified. My leg wasn't too painful—the shot went right through the meat of my leg and I don't know if there was shrapnel in there, but I had a hole in my leg. The navy medic ran a rod though the hole and that hurt worse than the shot. They cleaned it up and put iodine on it. O, mercy, that hurt! They loaded me on a B-47, and I woke up in a FEA-COM hospital in Tokyo. I was in a room with four other GIs."

The leg was wrapped and put in traction, but for some reason Ed had no pain. As he recalled that time he mused, "I think those spirits had protected me, so that I wasn't hurt any worse."

There was only a little throb in his leg, but he was hungry, and it seemed like forever before they fed him. He was there two days until the traction was removed. Bored, he put a robe over his pajamas and went down to the first floor where the PX, bar, dance hall, and restaurant were. "I was having a good old time until I got caught and ordered back to bed. They took my pajamas away, but in the same ward there was a fellow who had been run over by a tank and put back together with slings, splints, and wires—he was almost dead. Even though he couldn't move, he got clean pajamas every day, but he never used them, so I put them on and sneaked out again and had a good time running around Tokyo.

"One day a lieutenant came while I was in the hospital and he gave me a Purple Heart for being wounded in Korea. He said I had enough points to rotate home if I wanted to, but I was eighteen years old, had money in my pocket, and was game for more adventure, so I said, No—not yet.

"There were nine in the crew that went up that hill in Korea," Ed remembered. "Ray, a big hillbilly, and Cox, the oldest of the bunch, twenty-three, from New York. Elmer Lintz was there; he was a friend I went through basic with, and forward observer, and jungle survivor training. He was from Woodland, Nebraska—nice, quiet guy with one year of college, smarter than the rest of us.

"Lee, another operator with me, was also in the hospital but went back to duty and was killed." This was the first killing of a comrade that Ed experienced, and it dismayed and troubled him as no other death ever had. "He was just a kid—like me," Ed recalled decades later. "I think my ancestors were protecting me—they kept me alive."

Ed's air control officer, an Italian named Rudolph Valentino after the silent movie star, was killed a week after Ed was wounded in Korea. "It was tough knowing that guys I had served with and liked were dead. It was sad, and we survivors drank to forget how close death was to us."

After he was discharged from the hospital Ed went to Johnson AFB, forty-second fighter wing, and was assigned to a radar site at Komatsu, Japan, which now has a huge company that manufactures construction and industrial equipment. "First, I rode a bus from Tokyo, and then got on a train. Here I was, eighteen years old fresh off the rez, and I'm riding this train in the middle of Japan, nobody spoke English and a lot of them didn't like Americans—especially me—they called me a Nisei—a person who is half American and Japanese because I looked like that. I rode the train four days—barely moving, *dadoom dadoom*, though the mountains. Passengers had to bring their own lunch or buy from a gal that came through with rice cakes or soba noodle soup and Japanese beer that was the most terrible thing I ever drank. Hot sake was good, but if I drank too much of it really made me sick."

After four days he got off at Komatsu and walked up to the main part of town and got a cab. "The driver acted like he understood what I was saying, 'Air force base, base,' he nodded his head and said 'base,' and off we went. We went by rice paddies and I thought, Oh God, where are we going? This guy is kidnapping me. Then all sudden there was the base." It had originally been the Imperial Japanese Navy base, but the U.S. armed forces took over at the end of World War II. It had little maintenance, with only the center runway still useable although both sides were caved in and crumbling. The center was large enough for DC-6 or -3 and other small cargo aircraft to land. There were seventy-three men assigned to that base of Quonset huts. There were thirty-two to each hut, with sixteen on each side. Other huts were the orderly room and dining hall and there were hangers for special services. On top of the hill was the radar—the TPS 1B, run by electricity and turned slowly and didn't pick up much, but Ed guessed the radar crew was there to catch anybody trying to sneak into Japan. On July 27, 1953, the war was over. "I went to Tokyo met all the guys who were in our Korean outfit, and we celebrated big time."

Ed was back at Komatsu in the latter part of July or first part of August and found pleasant, temperate weather in a beautiful green area, a wonderful time of the year in Japan. The only negative was the reek of the rice paddies in the warm air; they were fertilized by human waste. His crew was pampered by maids, houseboys, cooks, waitresses—it was fun, enjoyable place to be for an eighteen-year-old who savored all the new experiences of his young life—so extremely different from Okreek, South Dakota. His crew met a Japanese woman whom they called "Mama San," and she called Ed Yoko, which was like Sonny. Ed guessed that she thought he was still a kid and needed such a nickname and his crew mates teased him about being a *Yoko.*

There were nine young radar operators at the base, and they had few responsibilities since there were no airplanes flying. They were bored. They made a sport of killing flies while on duty. Individual counted their kills—fifteen or twenty and other times up to fifty—there were so many of them. After hours, they drank fifteen-cent beers or got a bottle of whiskey for one dollar and five cents. The Japanese stuff was even cheaper. Ed and

A Kid in Uniform

his crew drank when they were off duty. "There wasn't much else to do," he recalled.

Ed also recalled that "In October 1953, all the U.S. armed forces realized they didn't need these troops now that the war was over, so they came out with the policy that anyone who had two years' service could be discharged—just about everybody went out. There were only three of us operators on the radar unit and we had to train someone new—bring him up to kill flies. I was okay being there, but it was hard on some of the others who were married and wanted to go home. I didn't, I was enjoying life too much.

"There was a kid who wanted to commit suicide. We were by the Sea of Japan and there was a fifty-foot cliff at the end of the runway; he stood on the edge the cliff and threatened to jump. The sergeant tried to talk him out of it, but after about two hours he got tired of it and told him, 'Okay, jump! You damn fool! Jump!' The kid jumped, but he landed on a ledge about twenty feet down and broke his leg. We had to call in a helicopter from Masuwa to pick up the kid and fly him out—I don't know what happened to him.

"When we weren't on duty, we played baseball, but we did not have nine Americans to make a team, so four Japanese played with us. We would go to the small towns around and play against their teams. Most of the time we got beat because they used a hard rubber ball instead of a standard baseball. When you hit it hard, it flattened—no longer round. The Japanese knew how to hit this kind of ball and most of the time beat us. Often after a game we were invited to the mayor's place and given a little sake or tea. That's where I ran into a guy who sold handmade tea sets from China. I paid five packs of cigarettes for a set and sent one to Carmen and to Virginia. Cigarette packs were the currency, not cash; a carton was $1.10, and one could buy the whole world over there with cigarettes.

"Mama San, the one who called me a Nisei, was the source for black market goods. We airmen would trade cigarettes for stuff we couldn't get otherwise. One time I got drunk in an upstairs bar and the Japanese police chased me up and down the stairs. Downstairs Japanese businessmen sat at a hibachi table—small and round—with their feet hanging below it. I grabbed a robe, sat down, and pretended to be one of them. The police didn't find me.

"A maid did our laundry and all household chores—we were well taken care of even though I didn't expect much, not when you're from Okreek or Mission, South Dakota—I was well pleased with being there.

"We bought a scooter big enough for four riders and we drive into town, we liked the Soba Café, where you could get good soup and noodles. It was run by this woman who was well educated and spoke good English, but she hated GIs. One day we took the corner too sharp and ended up in one of those stinking rice paddies—that woman got a kick out of that.

"We did a lot of hunting. At the end of the five-thousand-foot runway was a freshwater lake with reeds all around it and geese and ducks in there. The problem was we couldn't get buckshot and had to use size eight skeet shot to shoot ducks and it's hard to hit them, but we had fun trying. I tried putting oil in with the shot thinking that the oil would hold the shot together. I was behind the boat we used for hunting and pushed a barge ahead of us. A flock of ducks flew up in front of us, so I shot, over my friend's head, and then he hollered, 'I'm hit, I'm hit, I'm dying!' He felt the hot oil running down the back of his neck—he thought it was blood, but he had not gotten hit. We were alarmed and excited for a while, but it was funny too.

"There were swans in the lake, and we saw them swoop down to pull up the rice shoots the women were planning, so we started shooting at them—thinking we were helping the women. We killed one, but later found out that was not good. We had to apologize to the mayor for killing one of their sacred birds.

"We hunted in the thick cover grass in the embankments

the Japanese had built up to cover up their fighter Zeros and they were full of pheasants. We enjoyed hunting them. I was hunting one time with this kid from Hot Springs, Val Braddick, and we rode a scooter to the reeds at the end of the runway. When we looked out over the ocean, we spotted three big tornados, heading right towards the base. We jumped back on the scooter and sped the two miles to the base, yelling 'Tornado, tornado!' and set off the siren. Everyone came running to the orderly room Quonset and we pointed at the tornados. To our surprise they all laughed. What we thought were tornadoes were waterspouts. We didn't know the difference. They came over the base and dropped fish and frogs all over the grounds—they had been sucked up when the spouts were over the ocean. That was another exciting time."

In the fall of 1954, Ed played football. Every military base had a football team and there was stiff rivalry between them. On New Year's Eve, the command had a Rice Bowl and the winners of the teams from north and south of Japan, and another of Guam and other islands, played in the bowl. A call went out to the radar site at Johnson AFB asking anyone who had played football to try out for the teams. Ed liked football and he and others at the radar site played catch and pass games to relieve the boredom of their job. Ed got leave to go try out for the football team. He rode the train all the way down to Tokyo then got on a truck to Johnson AFB base where he checked in and had two weeks of calisthenics to get in shape. He was nineteen and weighed 210 pounds, which was too heavy. "I sweated out all the sake and beer I'd drunk while in Japan and made the team. I was down to 185 pounds and played second string defensive back, but mostly I sat on the bench, but I got to watch all the games. It was a do or die game—the commander sat on the end of the bench—and he would hoot and holler at the coach when the team made mistakes. We lost more games than we won and didn't make it to the Rice Bowl, but we had a big banquet celebration anyway."

Ed stayed on at Johnson AFB command center and enjoyed the easy duty even though it was sometimes boring since no enemy was going to attack them in the middle of Japan. He recalled that, "The army got mad at the air force because we were getting top quality people and the dumber—lower IQs— were going into the army. We had to take so many of them— Barnes was one of those—he was a helper boy. We sent him down for a bucket of steam at the end of the runway from the CQ that was on duty there. 'Barnes is on his way to get a bucket of steam from you. If you don't have any there send him on to someplace else.' About four hours later here come Barnes—he said, 'By the time I got back here all the steam had run out.' I later thought he was the smart one, we had to do his work while he was gone and all he did was run around with his bucket of steam.

"There was an old man—old to me, I was nineteen years old—most everybody there was no older than twenty-five— even the commanders were young yet, but this guy was an old retired World War II soldier who was just waiting out his time. He'd call from his post to say he was tired and had to go to sleep—so we'd send someone to relieve him. He had quite a time of it—until he went home to retire. I thought he was old—he was sixty and here I am now eight-four years old— boy I'd like to be sixty again."

Ed's crew passed time in many ways—even built model airplanes at the radar site for something to do—but he also studied all the time he was there. "I took college courses at night on the base. I remembered what Dad said about education—that it was important, and I knew had more to learn. I even took a Japanese language class and tried to understand the movies we saw in the town with no English subtitles."

In May 1955 it was Ed's time to rotate back to the United States and now he was eager to get home. Korea had not been too tough a duty even though it was in enemy territory and was where he was wounded, but it was wet, rainy, and cold all the time. Ed liked Japan and the easy duty and the new experiences. "There was this guy," he remembered, "Lee, who had a 'Moose,' which is what we called a Japanese woman who shacked up with a GI. He asked a buddy to go down to the woman's hut to get his gear out while he distracted her. He then climbed up on the truck that was hauling us out to catch the ship that would take us back to the U.S. But the woman — madder than hell—ran after the truck throwing rocks at her former boyfriend and shouting, 'Bad GI! No good GI!' But he got away.

"We were eleven days on a troop ship. Our assigned berth was with the Army First Cavalry unit in the warm kitchen, but the poor dogfaces were out in the cold as we sailed down the Aleutian Chain. We few airmen again got KP and were detailed to the mess hall, where it was warm and comfortable. It was a wet trip. The latrine had ten holes in the bow of the ship and we soon learned the best seats were in the middle—the water on the ones on the ends would slop over your bottom when the ship rolled.

"One thing I regret," Ed mused, "is that I didn't take pictures like some of the guys did. Others bought cameras in Japan and took all kinds of pictures of mountains just as beautiful as the Black Hills or Glacier National Park. There were quaint, lovely inns—hotels in the mountains with hot spas and fantastic scenery beautiful. Now, I wish I had pictures.

"We debarked at Seattle and I flew to San Francisco, where Mom met me. After I was in the air force and Virginia was in college, Mom married Lawrence Posey, who was a purser on navy ships."

Lawrence was originally from Oklahoma, a Creek Indian whose grandparents had walked the Trail of Tears from the Carolinas to Indian Territory in Oklahoma. His first wife was Dorothy Allen, from Flandreau, South Dakota, and they had one child, Larry John Posey. Dorothy died, leaving Lawrence with a two-year-old son to raise. His mother-in-law offered to take the boy for as long as necessary. Lawrence visited Flandreau as often as he could and was friends with Agnes and Harry Ross. Agnes was Dorothy's sister and Harvey, Mom's brother; they thought the two widowed people should get together and arranged a meeting. They clicked and were married and settled in Walnut Creek, California, near San Francisco, from where Lawrence sailed.

"Mom picked me up at the airport and she gave me the ride of my life down the freeway. It was my first ride on the freeway and a lot different than South Dakota's two-lane highways. She zoomed into Walnut Creek—cutting in and out of traffic—I couldn't believe this speedster was my mother. Her house sat up in the foothills of Mount Diablo and George and Delores Armstrong lived across the cul de sac and became good friends to Mom and Lawrence and later to Carmen and me. This was in 1954, the houses were new and in a desert setting and both lots needed landscaping. I went back in 1961 I couldn't believe the improvements they had made in the yards at Walnut Creek—grass, trees, shrubs, and flowers—it was beautiful.

"I was going to be stationed in Cut Bank, Montana, so I left Mom's and flew up to Portland, Oregon, and from there to Great Falls, Montana. I had never watched TV before so while I waited for my flight out of Portland I went into the bar and watched *Howdy Doody* and boxing matches. I was so engrossed I missed my plane and I had to stay over and fly out the next day. When I checked into Great Falls, I found that I had thirty days' leave coming so I took a train to Edgemont, South Dakota, and called my cousin Penny Conroy and she drove me to her home in Pine Ridge. I stayed overnight then got the bus to Mission where I stayed with Grandma and Grandpa Driving Hawk. Grandpa had an old pickup he let me drive, I went to Okreek to see Grandma and Grandpa Ross, and finally I went to see Carmen. It was as if I had never been gone. We picked up where we left off and planned to get married in August.

"It was a wonderful time—I stayed in Mission—good to see

A Kid in Uniform

all the relatives. After my leave was over, I rode the bus to Great Falls and from there to Cut Bank. I had to sit there all night and didn't wake up at five in the morning to catch the bus—I missed it two days in a row. So, when I did get there, I was two days AWOL. I saw the commander, Captain Wilson, and he said, 'I gotta do something with you,' so he gave me two weeks of labor to dig up an old sewer line. The radar site was forty-five miles out of town on the Canadian border—out in the middle of nowhere, wheat fields, nothing else. I worked every night on the sewer line and a local civilian contractor saw me toiling every evening, working hard as if I liked what I was doing. After my evening work on the bases ended, he hired me for a construction job he had, which I did after my base duties were done. I needed the money—I hadn't been paid in five months. My pay records were sent to Fort Bragg, North Carolina, with the army group I came home with from Korea. After I got off duty at the radar site, I worked two or three hours in the evening and earned a nice little nest egg.

"Finally, on July 1, my pay records caught up with me. I went and cried on the commander's shoulder about how much I was in love and I needed to go back to Mission to see my Carmen. He gave me a thirty-day leave and I went to Mission—we were going to get married."

3

Family

CARMEN WAS NINETEEN AND ED WAS TWENTY WHEN they were married on July 9, 1955, at two o'clock in the morning. They had been to the county offices in Winner, forty-three miles east for the license, but then had to find a priest to marry them. Carmen was Roman Catholic and wanted Father Hamuler, the priest at Mission, whom she had known and liked ever since she was a little girl, to do the ceremony. However, when he found out that Ed was not Catholic, he refused and sent them to Saint Francis Mission, twenty miles away, where Carmen had gone to school. But "No," said the priest. "Father Hamuler knows you, so go back to Mission."

Again, Father Hamuler said, "No" and back they went to Saint Francis. It was now two in the morning and most of the wedding party left them in Mission and went home when they came back from Saint Francis.

It took a while to rouse Father Hamuler from bed, but he dressed and said, "Well okay, so we can all get some rest." Sleepily, the priest asked Carmen if she would marry Edward, she said, "yes." The he turned to Ed and asked, "Will you, Edward—Jumping Hawk, Chasing Hawk, or whatever your name is—will you take Carmen to be your wife?" and they were married.

Carmen's brother-in-law Joe (Bad) Waln had arranged a party for them at an outdoor dance floor at Parmalee, twenty-two miles off. Okreek musician friends, Percy Red Buffalo, Manuel Night Pipe, and their five-piece band were signed up to play for the dance. "But," Ed and Carmen laughingly recalled, "after driving back and forth to Saint Francis, it was too late. All our friends were in bed."

The newlyweds stayed with Carmen's parents, Adele and Lloyd Boyd, in Mission for the remainder of Ed's thirty-day leave. To get to Cut Bank, they boarded a bus to Rapid City, rode another all the way to their first home. Ed had found a one-room apartment for twenty-five dollars a month. It had a refrigerator and a stove in the space where a closet would have been. The radar site was forty-five miles north among golden wheat fields ready for harvest, a beautiful spot located near Glacier National Park. The Cut Bank Creek and area around it was a favorite of big game hunters, anglers, and hikers. But Ed didn't have time to engage in any of these activities, which he always enjoyed, as he was too busy with his duties as radar supervisor, recording all the aircraft flights from the airbase.

The newlyweds joined a group of other young airmen and wives who lived in town. One of them found a stray kitten which they gave to Carmen to keep her company while Ed was at work. Two days later they woke up to find the kitten jumping around and foaming at the mouth—it had rabies. "I tried to catch it," Ed said, "but it leapt at me and I jumped clear over the bed. Carmen said, 'get it, you big chicken,' so I found a box, threw it over the kitten, and then managed to get it into a gunnysack. We took it to the police and fire department, and they killed it. They guys who gave it to Carmen were just being friendly—they didn't know it was rabid."

On the ride back and forth to the base, Ed noted thousands of jackrabbits on the prairie along the road. He took a .22 rifle along and shot them for the twenty-five-cent bounty per each one. The small change paid for their gas and tires on the old Studebaker Ed bought for thirty-five dollars. Ed worked the midnight shift and sometimes on the way home in the morning, he'd stop by the Milk River and catch trout for a meal.

As a newlywed and very much in love with his bride he did

not drink as much because they did not have much money. "As long as I didn't take that first drink, I was fine."

It was a small base with only a half dozen personnel, most like them—young newlyweds, and they all became close friends. They made their own fun and often shared potluck dinners. Carmen remembered a couple from Mobile, Alabama, who acted as if the Civil War was still being fought. When Carmen announced that she was pregnant the southern wife said, "I could never have a baby up North. My family would never forgive for giving birth up here among Yankees." Another time Carmen told of being in a café with some other military couples when she overheard the southern gal say to her husband, 'Well if you're not going to tell them to leave, I'm walking out of here!' She was referring to two black men who were sitting nearby. Carmen said she was glad when the woman left.

Ed and Carmen's first son, James, named after Ed's father, was born in the Cut Bank hospital in June 1956. There was no military hospital nearby and the air force would not pay for babies born off base, so Ed took a thirty-day leave and worked at the construction job to earn enough to meet the $312.00 hospital bill.

The winter at Cut Bank was bitterly cold and windy. The men who had guard duty on the base's fence line froze in minus-twenty-five-degree Fahrenheit temperatures with a wind chill of minus forty. "The base commander, Captain Wilson," Ed remembered, "called all the troops in from the line and said that even though there was a big NATO exercise on, he wasn't going to have his troops out there to freeze." He was the electronics officer on base—an important job, but because of his kindness, he was relieved of duty.

Ed was a radar supervisor on the DEW (Distant Early Warning) line, which ran all the way across the United States. Ed's team's duty was to track all northern incoming aircraft and especially Russian aircraft that might come over the North Pole into the United States.

Ed left the air force when his tour ended August 29, 1956, but he had to repair the U-joints on the old Studebaker before he started the 979-mile drive to Springfield, South Dakota, with Carmen and baby James as well as a bird, a dog, and three tires strapped to the top of the car.

Ed had fond memories of living in Springfield with Grandma and Grandpa Driving Hawk when his father had been ill and his mother had earned an associate's degree at Southern State Teachers College. Ed enrolled at the college with a football scholarship with credits from the two years of classes he had in the air force and took classes in engineer drawing and electronic repair, plus two math classes. All GIs lived in married student housing on the north side of the campus and Ed hunted whenever he could and kept all the young couples supplied with pheasants and ducks, which helped with food expenses.

Ed played quarterback on the college's varsity team. Most of the players were just out of high school and younger than him, but he was still quick and strong. In play, he caught the ball, then handed it off to the running back, who ran with it until they were swamped by the opposing offensive line. Southern had a poor win record.

The scholarship money paid Ed's school fees, but he had very little had cash for anything else. "I had applied for assistance from the GI Bill, but we waited and waited for the money to come, but it never did, and I knew I had to do something because now I had a family to support besides the college expenses. So, at the end of the semester, we discussed what to do and decided our best option was for me reenlist in the air force." He sold his text books, took Carmen to Mission, and rode the bus to Offutt Air Force Base in Omaha, where he reenlisted. He got a $900 reenlistment bonus and went back to Mission on a thirty-day leave. They stayed with Carmen's parents and spent time with Ed's grandparents and other relatives before they moved to his assignment at the Air Force General Surveillance Radar Station near Osceola, Wisconsin.

Ed and Carmen enjoyed living in the small village located in the beautiful Saint Croix National Scenic Riverway, a mecca for sportsmen who enjoyed fishing and boating. Carmen found work as a nurses' aide at the Saint Croix hospital, where their second son, Raymond, was born. Ed recalled, "I took Carmen to the hospital, but I had to stay home with Jim who was just a little over a year old and he and I sat in our apartment and waited for word of the baby's birth. I kept drinking coffee and Jim wanted some too, but I just gave him milk."

It was a hard birth; the baby was so big he required a forceps delivery, which caused brain damage resulting in a developmental disability. Big brother Jim was glad to have a little brother and has always been Ray's protector. As an adult, Ray lives with his parents and has been a joy as well a big physical help in their lives after Ed's health deteriorated, leaving him with little muscle strength. Jim will care for Ray after Carmen and Ed are gone.

Carmen wanted her parents to know the children so Ed took leave and the little family drove back to Mission for a short visit and persuaded Grandma Flora Driving Hawk to come back to Wisconsin with them. Robert had died, and Ed didn't like her living by herself in the little house with no running water, especially in the winter when it was heated by a woodstove. Flora enjoyed watching and playing with her great-grandson's little family for the winter, but come spring she had to go home.

Ed was a buck sergeant now, with better pay, but he drank it up. Every Friday night he got off early and with the other NCOs went to the club to drink, laugh, and start a weekend party. At the time, his need for drink overcame any responsibility he might have felt for what he was doing to his family. He spent what little money they had, which Carmen needed to feed and clothe herself and the two boys, on booze. Later, in his sober days, he shamefully recalled, "During that time, I did a despicable thing. I was down at the local bar and drank until I had no money. I remembered that Jimmy had cash from his paper route, so I went up to his room, got his money, and started down the back stairs. I fell, and the loose change scattered all over, clinking and bouncing down the stairs. Carmen and the kids laughed and picked up the money. I was sober enough to be ashamed of what I had done; I stayed home and went to bed. But the next day I got drunk again."

From Osceola they transferred to Sioux Lookout in Northwestern Ontario, Canada, a radar site the Americans had built and operated by the 915th Aircraft Control and Warning Squadron. Ed, with a wife and four children, was promoted to staff sergeant, one of the youngest at that time in the air force. In Canada, booze was cheaper at the NCO club and he had more time to drink, but still managed to do a good job as a radar supervisor. He did not think he had a problem because he was still able to function as a productive airman.

Sioux Lookout is an outdoorsman's heaven. It has great hunting and fishing and the family loved the place. Their third son, Butch, and only daughter, Lori, were born while Ed was stationed there. Jim, the oldest, loved to fish. As soon as the school bus stopped before the house, he jumped off and ran to get his gear and fish until suppertime. He was so proud when his catch was the evening meal.

Ed served as a guide for officers coming up from division and NORAD headquarters and was assigned duty as the boat dock manager and oversaw all the personnel, boats, engines, gas, and maintained the boats for fishing. It was a great time and he enjoyed fishing and serving as an "Indian" guide to many upper-ranking officers. They enjoyed using fly rods to hook brook trout and the plentiful bass. He did not drink as much off duty, but drank with the officers whom he guided, and became buddies with them during the time spent fishing and hunting.

In Rice Lake he and a friend were canoeing out among the many small island in Minnitaki Lake when they spotted a moose about fifty yards from shore, and shot at it. I fell, but got up and they quickly paddled to shore. It was gone, but they heard it bellow, followed it up a hill, and finally found it hung up in a dead tree fall. Ed killed it, gutted it, and dragged the huge carcass to the lake as his friend carried their gear. A wild, cold wind rose, roiled high waves much too high and rough for the canoe. They quickly made camp with a small flickering fire on the island in the meager shelter of the bush. They cut off slabs of moose meat and cooked it before the fire soon died in the stiff wind.

"Mercy, we were cold," Ed shivered as he remembered. "We huddled together, but I shivered so hard my teeth clattered. No one knew where we were, and I knew Carmen was worried. My friend was in worse shape than I was. I started praying, but I was sure we'd die."

"I now think my ancestors were looking after me because we stayed alive. We drank lake water, but were mighty hungry when the storm finally let up. We were out there four days and mighty hungry and we decided to paddle home. I was in the rear, exhausted and weak, and mercy, it was tough going, then I noticed my buddy was barely dipping his paddle. I yelled at him 'Can't you paddle harder?' He turned to look at me and I saw he was turning blue, was panting and hugging his chest. He mumbled what sounded like 'Can't, my heart.'

"I felt like someone had punched me, I was so shocked. 'Hang on!' I yelled and kept going although I was tiring. He had known before we went out that he had a heart condition, but hadn't told me. Of course, neither of us thought we'd have such a rough trip. I had to do most of the paddling and started praying again. When we neared the dock, I started yelling for help and luckily some men heard and ran to pull the canoe onto shore. My friend was barely conscious when he was rushed to the hospital. He recovered, but we were lucky to get back when we did. Now, I know for sure my ancestors had been taking care of me."

Ed had to have help dragging to moose home. "It had been

too cold for it to spoil, even though it almost killed us. I've never been so glad to see my family and get their warm hugs." With his sons' help he dragged the carcass to the basement, butchered and put it in footlockers and stored it on the front porch where it froze in the subzero temps. He carved chops off to eat and described it as "tasty, if lean—like very strong beef."

Ed was more cautious after that, checking his companions' health and the weather before going out, and never hunted so far out. He got a deer only fifty yards from the base, but it was an eerie experience when he saw wolves following them. "They were like shadows, following us through the woods—spooky and quiet but watching us. We were on snowshoes, slowly plodding through deep white snow, but kept an eye on them, but got a deer. We gutted it and cut it up to haul home. I looked back as we left, and those wolves were feasting on the guts we'd left in the snow."

He even shot a bear. He blew on a call that sounded like a wounded rabbit and lured a bear into shooting range. "I watched the woods in front of me, but heard trees rustle, turned around and there—only about a hundred yards away—was a bear. I shot and got it. We gutted it, skinned it, and cut it into meal-size cuts, hauled it home in the hide." Carmen and he cut and wrapped the meat and put it in the porch locker. "I salted the hide, rolled it up, and stuck it out on the porch to cure during the frigid winter. I was thinking of have a nice warm bear rug made, but when I unrolled it in the spring, I almost threw up at the stink of the rotten hide."

While Ed, in addition to his base duties, hunted and fished, Carmen kept busy caring for home and family, but also was an active member of the wives' club. The radar stations were usually located in small installations and so the line between officers and enlisted men was ignored and they cooperated to provide activities for all in the often rather isolated communities.

In Sioux Lookout Carmen helped organize a stage show

to benefit the Cree Indian children who lived nearby. "They were called First Nation people," Carmen remembered, "and they came quietly out of the bush—until suddenly they were in the yard with furs they wanted to trade. I invited them in for coffee and tried to visit with them, but they spoke poor English—or were shy. But after that first time I gave them coffee, they came back and brought us wild rice. The women paddled the canoes in among the wild rice beds, and the men pulled the stalks over the canoe and with a stick beat the heads into the bottom on the canoe.

"They were a poor people and often there were little kids without families. The Canadian government gave them a school where they stayed all year, but they didn't have much and we wanted to help them—and give us something to do." Carmen recalled that the wives' club decided to have a variety show as a fundraiser to help the poor tribe.

"We did it for two years, and at the first performance I danced the hula, but the next year I was big and pregnant with Lori and helped backstage. It was fun," she recalled. "The base captain did an impersonation of Victor Borge; there was barbershop quartet; a dance line did the Can Can, there was a hilarious comedian, and a husband and wife who did a parody of 'Stormy Weather.' There were twelve acts of songs and skits. Ed was a stagehand."

Their base housing was adequate, and she had a clothesline that she pulled out of a box and hooked to a pole in the yard. She kept an eye out for bears or other wildlife when she was hanging up clothes. The bears had gotten used to human food by pawing through the trash at the dump. "It was an interesting place to live—what with the animals, the Crees, and the Frenchmen who canoed the lake." In the winter, French loggers drove trucks over the thick ice with the season hauls of hewn trees.

But like all military postings, it was only temporary, and they moved next to Eagle Pass, Texas, for one year, which Ed described as the "worst duty anywhere." The base was a former World War II army training base with a runway that was fifteen miles from the town—hot dry, full of scorpions, lizards, and snakes. Carmen was afraid to let the kids play outside. Ed would take the boys in the car and let them take turns sitting on his lap and steering the car down the runway. There was no concern about any traffic. Ed took them fishing in the Rio Grande where they caught catfish, sturgeon, and alligator gar—which was the ugliest fish they'd ever seen. Ed also hunted and downed a javelina and a mountain lion.

Their house was just off the base and every evening, the kids would stand at attention and salute during the evening ritual as a bugle blew taps and the flag was lowered. One evening four young GIs ran off base to avoid the nightly ceremony but were soon caught. The commander ordered them to stand at attention and salute behind the Driving Hawk children for one week. The children were tickled and proud to set an example for the men. Then after President Kennedy's assassination, they sadly saluted while watching the solemn Change of Command ceremony attended by the whole base in dress uniform. "I had been on leave and didn't have time to get a haircut," Ed recalled, "so Carmen got her scissors and chopped away. There were straggly ends that I tucked up under my cap."

That was the start of Carmen being barber to Ed and her children and she became skilled at it and of course it was cheaper with four kids and Ed needing frequent trims.

Ed was next assigned to remote duty in Alaska as part of NORAD (North American Air Defense Command), a combined organization of the U.S. with Canada that provided aerospace warning. At first Carmen went back to Mission and stayed with her mother, Adele, for two months, but then went to her brother Dick's in Dallas, Texas. From there she and the children took the train to San Jose, California. It was a long trip with four children, but they enjoyed it—especially Butch, who soon figured out how to run the whole length of the train—from car to car.

Ed's mother, Rose, met them, and they drove to Walnut Creek where they lived with the Poseys while Ed was deployed in Alaska. Rose welcomed the company as her husband Lawrence was only briefly home between times at sea with the navy. It was to have been a short stay until Ed's return, but it ended up being a whole year. During that time Carmen had problems with her back and had surgery in the military hospital in Oakland. During the long hospitalization and recovery Rose cared for the children. Rose enjoyed her grandchildren, especially three-month-old Leo, the youngest of their four sons. Carmen remembered how distressed she was that the baby didn't know her when she came back from the hospital. She could not lift him until her back healed and he preferred his grandmother's arms to hers. When the family left to join Ed on his return to the States, Leo cried for Rose, and later, whenever she visited, he eagerly held out his arms to her.

In Alaska, without his family to worry about, whenever Ed had a three- or four-day break, he sat with other men—all with the same problem—in a room and drank. Sometimes they frequented a bar in King Salmon. When he rotated back from duty on the Aleutian Chain the crew went to the Montana Bar in Anchorage, which had a padded wall. "There were dwarfs that took five bucks from us drunks to throw them up on the wall. We had a contest to see which of us could throw the little men the highest." Forty years later, Ed noted, "Now I am very much ashamed for having been a part or such a foolish, ridiculous game."

In Alaska Ed took General Jimmy Doolittle fishing and recalled, "It was an honor for me to go with the U.S. Air Force hero who led a retaliatory air raid on Japan after the attack on Pearl Harbor, and I was sober when I took him out. But off duty I drank, yet I managed to maintain my position and responsibilities."

After a year in Alaska, Ed moved to McClellan AFB in Sacramento, California. Carmen and the four kids moved into a little house in North Highlands, near the base. He didn't fly as often a McClellan and took a job as a furniture salesman and earned good money, which he used to fund his drinking sprees. "But I didn't drink all of the time, and would often take the kids camping and fishing in the mountains."

Still Ed is now remorseful about that time. "I drank, not even thinking that I was an alcoholic and that it an incredibly costly disease. Many times, after I was arrested for drunk driving, I was let off because I was between tours in Vietnam or the judge dismissed the case with a minimum charge and fine because I had to go back to the war. There had been other times back in Osceola where the judge and officers knew me and so they let me off with a minimum fine. I was lucky—or maybe the spirits were watching over me, but it was still costly. The worst cost was the loss of friends that could not put up with my drinking. They could be friends with Carmen, but they could not stay when I was around."

One time after he had flown a mission, Ed stopped at home long enough to change clothes and then headed to a bar. He has no memory of how long he was there nor who he was with, but came to on a bus not knowing how he had gotten there. He got off in Oakland and hailed a taxi to go to Walnut Creek, not even asking about cost, and the driver was thrilled, and they arrived at to his mother's house at two in the morning, but with no money to pay for the taxi. He woke Rose and Lawrence, who paid the fifty-dollar cab fare. Rose was appalled at Ed's condition but led him into house, gave him coffee, and put him to bed. He slept all that night, but was so sick in the morning that he stayed in bed and slept all the whole day. Then they took him back to Sacramento.

As usual, Carmen was waiting for him, just as if nothing had happened, not even asking, "Where have you been, are you in trouble?" Ed recalled. "But Mom and Lawrence scolded me and never let me forget that I owed them fifty dollars. I did not blame them—it was something that should never have happened. Again, I was ashamed of myself, but not enough to stop drinking."

On one of his drunks, Carmen hosted her church women's group from the base for their monthly meeting. She cleaned house and moved the couch to other side of the room. Ed did not know that and when he entered the room, he smiled, introduced himself and went to sit where the couch usually was but plopped on the floor instead. Embarrassed he got up and said, "Carmen, if that is what you are going to do, I'm not going to stay here," and slammed out the door to get drunk.

Carmen was a devoted mother, taking care of the baby, Leo, and the three older kids, in addition to working outside the home to supplement Ed's allotment pay. Now he marvels why she put up with his binges and blackouts, when he would be gone for days. When asked why she did it, she replied, "I loved him and knew that he was a basically a good man. And I prayed. Maybe I should have kicked him out then, but I couldn't raise the kids alone." She took the children shopping with her and warned them, "Now, stay close. If you get lost, you'll have to walk home."

Butch had to go to the restroom and when he did not come out Carmen was alarmed. There had been reports of a child molester in the vicinity, so she called the police. They searched the area and sent Carmen home with the other kids so they'd know where to reach her. She was so worried, but when she got home, there was the lost boy waiting for her, "Hi, Mom," he said, "What's going on?"

He had come out of a different door at the restroom and didn't know where he was. He searched, but when he didn't find his mother he did what she had told him to do—walk home—all seven miles.

Butch seemed more adventurous than the other children. He liked to ride his trike on the sidewalks in the neighborhood. One time he spotted smoke coming out of a neighbor's garage, so he sped down to the local firehouse to report it. He was hailed a hero by the firemen and got a ride in the big truck and awarded a certificate of appreciation. When they moved back to South Dakota, he discovered a loophole in the state's election law, which allowed an eighteen-year-old to run for governor. In 1978 he campaigned but did not make it through the primaries.

Ed often passed out and then awoke in the morning, knowing that he had spent all the money he had, leaving none for Carmen and the kids. "I would be mortified at what I had done and even though I was also dreadfully sick, I did it all over again. I have been sober for forty years and appreciate how lucky I was to get through the alcoholic years—much of it I do not remember. That part of my life is totally gone. It had to be my ancestors watching over me."

At McClellan, Ed was pleased to get flying status, which paid better. He was flying in an EC-121, a World War II aircraft converted to a spy plane with radar plus control capabilities. His crew's initial duty was to fly an oval racetrack pattern over Vancouver, Canada, looking for Russian aircraft. He had more training to be an airborne radar aircraft control officer and learned all the parts of the airplane and took a miniature flight school to learn to fly the plane in case the pilot was incapacitated. After the training, his group had a change of command and with it, different operational duties. He enjoyed the duty at McClellan, where he trained new young airmen. "One time this new kid was late to duty, but had a note from his mother, asking that he be excused because he had overslept. Just like he was still in school."

During the Cuban crisis, before Kennedy was assassinated, Ed's crew flew out of Orlando, Florida, to Cuba with fighter aircraft cover at 35,000, their unarmed plane flew about 150 feet above the water into Cuba and across the island trying to entice the Russian MiG-21 aircraft to scramble out of their twelve-mile-radius protected zone. If one of the MiGs flew out of the area, the radar men instructed the fighter planes to fire at them. "We took off at 0430 to get to Cuba in the early morning when the MIGs scrambled. We hoped they would follow us, but they never did, and our side never got a shot." They flew nineteen missions over Cuba.

In February 1963, they flew a mission out of Panama to keep radar control over the fighter aircraft escorting President Nixon on his tour of Japan. Their next mission was in Hawaii, where they tried to spot the Russian Sputnik on radar and recover it before the Russians did. They waited around four days until finally, Sputnik came out of orbit, "but we missed it by seventy-five miles and the Russians recovered it."

On October 1964, there was a large earthquake in Alaska, which caused severe damage and killed over one hundred people. It also knocked out all the radar sites on the DEW line. Ed's crew was on standby until ordered to grab their toothbrushes and fly out. They wore light summer uniforms and about froze to death while up there in the arctic cold. Their duty was to provide a radio relay system for all the land-based radar stations, which had lost contact in the quake. "They would call us and then we radioed on to the command post."

He was still drinking but managed to always do his duty.

4

Vietnam

BACK AT MCCLELLAN AFB, THERE WAS NOT MUCH activity for Ed's crew until 1964–65, when they went on alert. "We were ordered to fly so I said goodbye to Carmen and the kids, but couldn't tell her where we were for going, but we knew that it was probably Vietnam. We flew sixteen hours to land on Midway Island. I could not imagine that there had been a battle there during World War II because it was just a big old sandbar, but it was part of the chain of islands fought over in the war. There were still ruins and battle artifacts littering the land and in the sea. While there, we laughed at the gooney birds that bounced and rolled as they landed. That was the only island where we saw those birds. They were big round balls of feathers all over the runway and we had to chase them off before we could take off."

Ed watched the landscape flow by under the plane's first flyover of his beginning tour in Vietnam. It seemed an endless dark green of thick jungle interspersed with the lighter green of what looked to be pastures, but he found out later it was sharp-bladed elephant grass that the ground troops hiked through. After landing he climbed out of the plane into oppressive heat and humidity and gagged at the rank odor of stagnant water and rotten leaves mixed with the sickening sweet smells of strange, beautiful flowers.

In 1968 Ed viewed the war, which was not going well for the U.S., from the air. More than a half a million U.S. troops were deployed, and the death rate rose to 16,899, about 46 troops a day. In 2018, there are still 1,200 Americans unaccounted for and in China, Cambodia, and Laos 350 more men are missing.[1]

The radar crew's mission was named "Rolling Thunder." Their staging base was Taiwan, just across from China and they flew in an unarmed RF-101 and RF-4C photo-reconnaissance plane. There was an M16 rifle on board and each man carried a .38 pistol. "We never fired on the enemy but used our guns to kill rats that got into our quarters. They were as big as dogs. Once at four thirty in the morning I woke up to this guy screaming 'God damn it's in my bed!' He started shooting and we all pulled our guns and aimed at the rats—making a hell of a racket. The alarms sounded and here come the MPs who made us pick up all the bodies, but not all were dead, and one guy got bit. It was a hell of a night."

There were two Rolling Thunder air crews with separate barracks, and each maintained a plane. They alternated flights to Vietnam, landing at Tan Son Nhut AFB near Saigon, which was a Republic of Vietnam facility and the U.S. used it as a major base during the war. Radar missions became necessary after nine F-105 aircraft were shot down on their first bombing raid. MIGs scrambling out of China caught them unawares over North Vietnam.

"We flew early in the morning to fly over target areas immediately after a bombing raid to photograph the damage so that attack assessments could be made."

In addition to the MIGs, Surface to Air Missiles (SAM) were launched without any warning, which led to loss of planes and men. "Our job was to spot them on radar," Ed explained, "and to warn our bombers. We also jammed the SAM system to ensure that our fighter aircraft would not go in the no-fly zone or fly into China. That was our main concern. We were under the direct command of the U.S. Joint Chiefs of Staff.

"We rotated missions with the other crew to fly ten missions. Sometimes, we rotated in six or seven days, but other times it would be three weeks before we would get our ten missions done. We would take off from Tan Son Nhut about 4:30 a.m., fly four hours to Da Nang, refuel, then fly through Laos across North Vietnam. We took photos to show that the bombing raids were effective and not in a no-fly zone. On another route we flew over the gulf of Tonkin, entering VC territory, and flew over the Hotel Hanoi."

There were many frightening incidents on the missions they flew in their unarmed plane. "We often took enemy fire and I believe my ancestors were protecting me–'cause we always made it, even when our plane was hit. One time we flew to our station and were following our bombers and taking pictures of their hits. On radar I picked up a MIG that had scrambled out of Hanoi. I called Major Derby, out aircraft commander, and reported the MIG about twenty miles off.

"'Keep me in formed,' he said.

"'Ten miles,' I said.

"'Roger.'

"'Five miles,' I reported.

"'Roger,' Major Derby said and put the plane in a straight down drive. The max speed for that plane was 310 knots and at that speed the wings might come off. I knew we were over max when we zoomed down. I expected to crash, and I tried to get up to the back door where I could exit, but we were at such an angle it was like climbing a steep ladder and I could not get there."

"Major Derby pulled up over treetops, evaded the MIG, and flew between mountains on either side of us and we were low enough to see trees in the valley. We flew in radio silence at that altitude all the way to Da Nang and all the while mortars banged away at us. Major Derby yelled, 'Let's get out of here!' We flew and flew I didn't think we'd ever get there, but now I believe my ancestors were protecting me."

Ed recalled that Major Derby asked, "Shouldn't we be over the Philippines by now?"

"The navigator said, 'We should be, but I don't see it.' He

could not find the Philippines! We got a radio beacon on the radar and turned around to the Philippines. That navigator was not too good—on some of the missions, he was drunk. He was a WWII recall and his previous duty had been running the officers' club—he should have stayed home.

"One of the worst things about out missions—other than drawing ground fire—was when we all had dysentery—terrible diarrhea. We had a saying, 'a dry fart was heaven.' It was terrible when we had to fly. On our first mission after we lifted off from Tan Son Nhut, Major Derby crapped his pants and he had to sit in it for four hours. Many of the crew also had it—what a mess—it really stunk.

"At Da Nang, there were potty houses—just holes in the ground to squat over. Major Derby stopped the aircraft there and the men bailed out and ran to the squat holes. It was a stinking mess in that hot, steamy climate, with no showers and we were filthy. The whole area stunk of mold, shit, and rot." Their quarters were hutches, a permanent thatched hut with screens that they called "hooches." Each crew had its own hut and there were two hundred army men and marines plus Ed's group living in the hooches.

Ed's crew completed three six-month tours of Vietnam and flew 156 missions. In between missions Ed's crew waited in the monotonous heat, bored, reading the same old books, playing endless games of pinochle and slapping mosquitoes. The nights were cold, and they were never dry in the monsoon season's unending curtains of rain. "The army and marines were into pot and drugs in the jungle. We airmen drank."

It was after his second tour in Vietnam that alcohol became a real problem at home. He had to have his drink, and Carmen was getting tired of him spending his pay on binges and blackouts, often not knowing where he was. She was pleased when Ed's commander called about another tour. "Ed doesn't have to accept this—he's had two tours in Nam—but if he wants, he can have a third tour."

Carmen readily agreed, "I know he wants to go," knowing that when he was on duty, he had to stay sober to fly and he would earn combat pay, which would help the family's economic situation.

When Ed staggered home after an all-night binge, she handed him his gear—all packed—and hustled him to the base. Ed was so soused he passed out on the plane and awoke, hungover and sick, on a troop transport plane. On the ground he groaned, recognizing the hot steamy jungle, but as soon as he could after checking in, he rushed to the base bar. As much as he needed it, alcohol still did not prevent him from doing his job.

Where ever Ed was stationed Carmen was always involved in airmen wives' activities. At McClellan Carmen made a point of organizing the young wives of airmen who were in Vietnam. The base commander had told them not to tell outsiders where their husbands were, lest they be harassed by antiwar factions who often publicly booed and shouted angrily, "You commie lovers! Your husband are god damn baby killers!"

Sometimes a lonely wife was called in the middle of the night and heard an anonymous voice asking, "Do you know where your husband is?" then when the wife did not respond the voice said, "He's killing babies in Vietnam."

Carmen started a support group for the young airmen's wives with the base commander's support. She and an officer made a point of checking on the women's well-being. One time they went to the residence of young wife who had recently given birth.

Even before they knocked on the door, they heard the baby wailing. They knocked harder and called the girl's name. "Open up!" There was no response and the officer kicked the door open. Inside the baby lay on the floor, in a soiled diaper. It chewed on its fist and wailed. The mother sat near the baby, staring vacantly into space. not responding to the baby nor the officer and Carmen. The young girl had cracked under the strain of insensitive, cruel baiting about her "commie-loving husband."

To help build the wives' morale, Carmen and the base chaplain organized a bus trip to San Francisco where the they visited Fishermen's Wharf, a wax museum, and had lunch. It was a relaxing, carefree outing, which they enjoyed without being publicly jeered and booed because their men were in Vietnam. "It was a hard time," Carmen recalled, "but we became a real close group and helped each other in many ways."

In Vietnam Ed was now responsible for four young radar operators and controllers who were only eighteen or nineteen years old. "I was twenty-nine but was a father figure to those boys as well as counselor, chaplain, and their boss. It was a terrifying time for them, and even in my drunken state, I had to make sure those kids came back okay. I think we did our jobs because we were too scared to be cowards."

Ed proudly received five air force medals for meritorious achievement while participating in aerial flights over Vietnam. Two of them were for aircraft bombing, another for flying along the Cambodian border when the B-52s were bombing the VC to make sure they did not drop them in Cambodia. "They flew an EC-12 at sixteen thousand feet and the bombers were at thirty-five thousand and it seemed like they were right on top of us—it was frightening. However, we completed the mission and made sure the bombs landed in the right places."

There was a radio station on a mountain peak in North Vietnam that stuck straight up in the air and was so steep that the VC could not scale it. Channel 96 was its call signal and it was the focal point for U.S. aircraft to calculate their distance from the MIGs. "We checked to notify all the navy and air force aircraft that we were ready for business. Our bombers gave their call signs and many times, the MIGs waited for the bombers or scrambled and went back to China. One time they scrambled out of Hanoi, but a navy pilot latched on to one of the MIGs and followed it into China. He shot it as it descended to land. That created quite a stink because he was not supposed to fly into China. The Joint Chiefs of Staff had to see the films we had taken of the incident to answer China's complaint."

At another time, an F-111 with radar flew over mountainous terrain without running into anything—it just rode over the peaks. However, on its first mission, an F-111 flew into a mountain, and the second plane landed too soon, and it crashed—so three F-111s were lost in two weeks. Again, the radar showed the films to see how it happened. The air force soon discontinued the used of F-111 planes.

The radar crew shot moving pictures from an EC-121, but also still photos of the Ho Chi Min Trail. The jungle path was the main supply route for the VC and was a target for U.S. planes to knock it out of use. Photos indicated that it had been destroyed, but next day the camera view showed that it was being used again—as if nothing had happened to it. The coolies, who lived along the road, repaired it soon after it was bombed. Manual labor kept it open.

Ed recalled, "The most satisfying thing we did was to pick up the radio signals of downed U.S. pilots and directed rescue choppers to them. We circled overhead and we stayed in the area until we knew they were safe. Of course," Ed quietly said, "not all of them were rescued and we sometimes watched as they were captured or shot and there wasn't a damn thing we could do. That was tough, but those who were rescued thought we were heroes.

"Still, our main mission was to jam the North Vietnam radar so that it could not launch a SAM. On my first tour, we manually cranked the height finder as fast as we could to keep the SAM from launching and blowing us out of the sky. One time our antennae stuck 'cause it was so wet and rainy. We'd pull and jerk and finally the pilot turned the plane and aimed the props at the radio shack to try to dry it. The guys working there came piling out—they about blew the whole thing over—but it worked. We successfully jammed all the North Vietnam's equipment."

The Tet Offensive took place in January 1968. Ed's crew sat in their hooch playing pinochle on a piece of plywood for a table. Suddenly, they heard the scream of mortars—they were under attack! "We scrambled out, I stepped on the plywood, and it flipped over this guy lying by it. We all ran out the door until he hollered, 'Hey, wait for me!' We dug him out of there and ran out. Two air police ordered us to get into our plane. Major Derby was revving the engine and when the whole crew was on, we raced down the runway—luckily not shot up—and took off. There was a curtain of ground fire tracers all around us, but we made it. The other flight crew was caught, and two men were wounded—one badly hurt. We flew to Taiwan and laid up there because the command canceled our flights because of the danger of being overrun again."

After they had flown ten missions over Vietnam, the crew returned to Tan San Nhut and got a call from headquarters to fly into Pleiku and pick up some fourth army division casualties. The division had landed in Vietnam and set up for the night, but for some reason very few guards were posted. It was not too far from the Cambodian border and the VCs launched an attack and practically slaughtered the whole fourth division. There were so many casualties the unit was unable to evacuate their dead and many bodies lay in body bags lining the runway. The main aircraft flew the wounded out to the Philippines and Tan Son Nhut or to Germany, but the radar plane was needed to fly out the dead. They landed and began loading the body bags. Ed's voice was somberly quiet as he told, "It was an overwhelmingly sad yet nauseating duty. We loaded fifteen decomposing bodies and felt them sloshing about when we lifted the bags and we tried to be gentle and respectful as we loaded them onto the plane. It was tough because all the while, our men were gagging and throwing up. We carried the dead back to Tan Son Nhut, unloaded them on the runway in unbearable heat. It was an excruciating, miserably rough job, but we did it.

"At that time," Ed said, "I did not know our cousin Bunky Anderson was a first sergeant in the fourth division—Dennis Anderson was his name and he was from Omaha. His mother was Arlene Raymond, Mom's first cousin. I went back a long away with Dennis. When Ted Roulliard and I were the two smallest boys at Hare School, Aunt Arlene bought Dennis and asked me to watch out for him and take care of him, 'because he was kind of a smart little character.' He was part Indian but was a small and blond-headed kid that the bigger Indian boys liked to pick on—so Ted and I kept an eye on him and kept others from bullying him.

"At Christmas, after I was home from Vietnam, I learned that Bunky died with the fourth division in Pleiku, slaughtered by the VC. To this day, I still wonder if his body was in one of the bags we carried out of there. It is still hard for me to recall that time because I remember him as mischievous little kid at Hare School and he was still just a youngster when he died.

"After I was home, I heard that another cousin, Larry Lapointe, Aunt Dolly's son, died in Vietnam. Our family had a sad presence in that awful war."

Ed's crew spent lot of their time in Vietnam idly waiting around, especially during the Christmas holidays. "The command called a truce and we sat around for four or five days, waiting until the truce was over or one side violated it." Bored to tears, they drank until they could forget where they were.

Excitement filled the camp at Christmas because Bob Hope came to entertain the troops. To ensure the star's safety, four stages were erected in different places to confuse the VC so they would not know which one to attack. The stage on which he performed was on a flatbed truck and not too far from Ed's hooch, "so we got seats right up front. I was lucky to be so close and really enjoyed Bob Hope. It was the last show he did for the troops on Christmas. I do not know how long he had done this during WWII, Korea, and Nam, but he was popular with the troops.

"In Vietnam, we did our jobs, but also had the opportunity to feed our alcoholism. One time our copilot was so drunk he could barely make out the weather brief on the aircraft without falling asleep. Major Derby, the pilot, was skilled enough to fly the missions without our copilot. It was the same way with our navigator—a boozer—half the time he did not know what he was doing. I drank but was still able to do my job."

Ed had many exciting yet perilous experiences. Outside of flying in an unarmed plane and being the frequent target of enemy fire, one of the most perilous events—although he didn't know it at the time—was the exposure to what Ed always referred to as "that damn Agent Orange." It was an herbicide and defoliant chemical used as part of the U.S. Military's Operation Ranch Hand's herbicidal warfare program from 1961 to 1971. Helicopters and planes sprayed it over the jungles to kill the leaves and expose the VCs in the jungle below. When Ed's plane flew over the forest now, it was no longer green, but a gray area of bare dead trees. Ed remembered the time they landed at the base on Da Nang when all was total chaos under enemy mortar fire. The crew handling the filling of the air tankers, let the flipping hose get away and sprayed Agent Orange all over the men and planes in the area. Ed's crew was drenched before they could get off the ground.

Ed didn't know of its toxicity until years later in 1985 when he woke up at home in screaming agony and could not walk. Carmen called an ambulance which took him to the VA Phoenix hospital. They could do nothing for him, so he was flown to Williams Air Force Base hospital, and then to General Bowman Hospital in El Paso, the orthopedic military veteran's hospital. He was there for forty-five days, had shots of painkillers and steroids to numb the pain—he could not stand alone. There were many other veterans lying in anguish, their vertebras melting away, and nothing helped them other than shots and pills to numb their pain—they were dying. They did not know what caused it, and then the chaplain came to Ed and whispered, "Sir, you need to know that your illness was caused by Agent Orange even though the government hasn't admitted it."[2] When Ed got home, he had to learn to walk all over again. Carmen's mother, Adele Boyd, was visiting and she took his arm and helped him walk. They started out slowly down to the end of the driveway, then the block and finally all the around the block. It was six months before Ed could move on his own.

In 1986 or 1987, the U.S. government admitted that Agent Orange had caused many cancers. "Every one of my crew is dead, except me—I am still hanging in there," Ed sadly recalls. "The young crewmembers, who thought of me as a father figure, died in their early thirties—too young—because of that damn Agent Orange. Major Derby and older aircraft personnel lived to be about sixty before they perished. I had cancer of the testicles and of the kidney. I had to have a kidney removed in 1997 and that was when I had that wonderful strange near-death experience."

Ed survived the surgery and rehab, but needs to use a wheelchair, has episodes of intense pain, and cannot stand cold temperatures—even air-conditioning bothers him. In hot Arizona afternoons, he sits in the shade of the patio rather than in the cool house. When he's suffering so much, he says, "I often think about my vision where I had no pain and it was safe and warm but know—for some reason—it is not time to go there."

On one mission in Vietnam, Ed's crew had a rough landing off the runway into the mud and men were tossed all over the plane. "The tail was up about thirty feet in the air. I flew up, came down, hit my jaw on the radar console, and cracked all my teeth on both sides. I went to the dentist at Tan Son Nhut AFB and had to have all my teeth rebuilt. They lasted twenty years. A good thing about getting my teeth fixed was that it verified my tour in Vietnam and exposure to Agent Orange, which qualified me for the disability pay."

Sadly, Agent Orange caused the death of many veterans and the government can never give enough compensation for the use of that horrible chemical.

Ed joined the air force on August 29, 1952, and retired November 30, 1972, with an honorable discharge at KI Sawyer Interceptor Squadron, Marquette, Michigan. He has every right to be proud of "my twenty years, two months and seventeen days of active duty." For that service, he won the following awards:

Entitled Command Aircraft Control Specialist
Republic of Vietnam medal ribbons
Air Force Commendation Medal with four oak leaf clusters
Vietnam service medal
Air Force Longevity medal
Good Conduct medal with an oak leaf cluster
Five air medals
Two air force accommodation medals
Korean Service ribbon
United service ribbon
Combat Readiness medal

"I am proud of those medals, and proud of my tours in Vietnam, even though it was a rough time and exposure to the Agent Orange left me disabled; but also amazed that I did my duty even while I was drunk, but I am not proud of being an alcoholic."

Returning from Vietnam he had a raise in pay but was drinking about a fifth of bourbon a day plus a six-pack of beer to chase it down. Back in California he wanted to quit flying because he had to stay sober to fly stateside. He submitted a request to end his flying status and for an assignment on the ground. He first went to little place up in North Dakota, a base in a grain field in the middle of nowhere. When he pulled into the gate a young lieutenant greeted him and then signed Ed out because the base had closed. He was transferred to Duluth, Minnesota, but there was no job for him, so he transferred back to Osceola, Wisconsin, which was the best place to raise children and to have a good life. "It was an ideal spot for an old drunk because I had buddies to drink with—the base commander who was a pilot I had flown with in Vietnam, and two other vets all with the same problem. We opened the pub where we drank on our own time until finally, Carmen had enough, 'That's it!' and kicked me out. She was tired of my drinking, not having enough money, and was no longer going to follow me from base to base."

The base commander was relieved of his command because of his drinking so he, Ed and two other sergeants were transferred. Ed went to Volk Field, Wisconsin, which was a relief base for fighter aircraft. All he had to do was supervise five others to make sure they monitored the nuclear alarm codes. He had time to go into the local bars, drank his way through them, and did not show up for work for five days.

After this five-day drunk, Major Brecknor, Ed's commander and a pilot he had flown with in Vietnam, called Ed in and said, "Ed, this has got to stop! You got to quit this drinking and trying to work. Either you must give up the booze or—even with fourteen years in the service—you will have to get out of the air force." Ed respected Major Brecknor, who was a brave and honorable man. He flew combat missions in a DC-21 from an aircraft carrier until he was shot down, captured, and in POW camp until the end of the Vietnam conflict. He survived the camp, retired in Colorado, but died in a car accident in 2008.

When Ed decided to leave the air force Major Brecknor wrote a reference letter for him, which he might need for future employment.

To Whom It May Concern:

This letter is written for the purpose of introducing Mr. Driving Hawk and attesting to his capabilities and proven past performance. I have known Mr. Driving

Hawk, both personally and professionally, for two years. During this time he worked directly for me in a position of great responsibility and vital importance to our national defense.

From September 1970 to June 1971, Mr. Driving Hawk, then a Technical Sergeant, United States Air Force, was the supervisor of the Combat Alert Center at the Air Defense Command operational facility under my command. During this period, the unit manning was critically low and had to be augmented from personnel outside the unit on a temporary basis. This turbulence in essential personnel further aggravated a desperate manning problem and increased the pressure under which the Combat Alert Center people worked. The excellent sustained performance during this period by the Combat Alert Center is directly attributable to Mr. Driving Hawk. His complete and thorough knowledge of his job insured mission accomplishment; his deep personal understanding of people with and for whom he works created an atmosphere of cooperation and fostered esprit de corps.

From June 1971 to present, Mr. Driving Hawk has continued his outstanding performance. Mr. Driving Hawk possesses great integrity, he is of the very finest moral character, an extremely dedicated family man, and is extremely fair in his dealings with subordinates. He is an indefatigable worker with tremendous perseverance; he completed his college education while maintaining his outstanding duty performance. Mr. Driving Hawk's accomplishments, demeanor, and character remained superb even though he has endured great personal and family hardships. I believe this man is capable of rising to any occasion, accomplishing any objective, and enhancing any venture by his presence. He is an extremely stable, conscientious, and personable individual of great value to any organization. He is a solid citizen, a welcome member to any community, and an exceptionally fine human being. I highly recommend him for service, employment, or position in any organization.

MJ. William J. Brecknor Jr. Major USAF

Major Brecknor told Ed he had to quit drinking or be discharged from the air force. "I'm sending this man to pick you up tonight and take you to an organization called Alcoholics Anonymous." Ed did not know what that was but knew Brecknor was serious and Ed knew he had to quit drinking if he wanted to stay in the service and get Carmen and the kids back. After two weeks of going to AA meetings every night with his sponsor, George Segerstrom, Ed stayed sober. But he recalled, "It really did not soak in that I couldn't drink at all any more. I asked George if they had a pill to give me that I could take, but still drink and be all right. He laughed at me, 'The only pill you got is to stay sober and go to these meetings.' Old George stayed with me through the delirium tremens of alcohol withdrawal. God, it was awful. Saw snakes, evil things. I was cold, hot, shivered, hollered and cried!"

There is no cure for alcoholism, but Ed found a solution to his addiction in AA in the company of other men who were drunks who had to get sober—or else. They understood each other, the power of drink over their minds and bodies, and in the weekly meetings they supported and encouraged each other to follow the Twelve Steps not only during recovery, but for the rest of their lives.

AA Twelve Steps

1. We admitted we were powerless over alcohol—that our lives had become unmanageable.

2. Came to believe that a power greater than ourselves could restore us to sanity.

3. Made a decision to turn our will and our lives over to the care of God as we understand Him.

4. Made a searching and fearless moral inventory of our selves.

5. Admitted to God, to ourselves, and to another human being the exact nature of our wrongs.

6. Were entirely ready to have God remove all these defects of character.

7. Humbly asked Him to remove our shortcomings.

8. Made a list of all persons we had harmed and became willing to make amends to them all.

9. Made direct amends to such people wherever possible, except when to do so would injure them or others.

10. Continued to take personal inventory and when we were wrong promptly admitted it.

11. Sought through prayer and meditation to improve our conscious contact with God, as we understood Him, praying only for knowledge of His will for us and the power to carry that out.

12. Having had a spiritual awakening as the result of these Steps, we tried to carry this message to alcoholics, and to practice these principles in all of our affairs.[3]

Every time Ed craved a drink, he thought of Carmen, his fourteen years of service, and Major Brecknor was there to encourage and support him and Ed was determined to stay sober.

After three weeks, Ed was amazed how well he felt—physically and mentally better than he had in a long time. "I believe I had been insane as an alcoholic—mentally as well as sick with a terrible disease." Now that he was sober, he regretted the wasted years and money spent on drink. He called Carmen. "I've quit drinking for good. I'm sober and attending AA meetings, can I come home?" He was so thankful when she said yes. He went to Osceola to see her and the kids. It was a joyful reunion but when Ed asked her to move down to Volk with him she said, "Let's give it another month—if you're still sober then I'll bring the kids down." He stayed sober another month and Carmen and the kids moved to a new home in Shell Lake, Wisconsin.

It was a good time, the kids had fun fishing and Ed loved having his family with him. They found a farmhouse in the country with a big yard. Ed got the kids a little electric bike on which they zoomed around open fields, having a great time. "They went to school—we had a happy time because I was sober."

Ed faithfully attended AA meetings with a great group of men—all old drunks. "One guy drove a semitruck and finally had to give up drinking because he no longer could drive when he was drunk. Then there was a guy who owned gas stations and he could no longer maintain the pumps when drunk and had to sober up or lose his business." There were others his age or older, but also a couple of young men whose families had intervened to get them out of the drinking cycle. "We were all there for the same reason—to stay sober. We went to meetings once a week and once every month all the families would get together to have a buffet with a delicious barbecue. One time it was so delicious, but I didn't know what I was eating, beef or pork and the cook said it was raccoon—the first time I ate raccoon."

Ed helped start a halfway house and a drug treatment program adjacent to Shell Lake, the hospital where he became acquainted with all the doctors and helped them hire the necessary counselors. He found it to be interesting and challenging work to organize such a program. At the same time, he volunteered to work as a planner for the Saint Croix tribe, a small band of three thousand members and worked on many programs with the Lac du Flambeau tribe.

He became friends with the men who took him fishing during the spring walleye spawn. "We'd walk down to the river at night and watch for these big fish to rise and then spear them. They were fifteen- to twenty-pound fish. Fabulous!

"In the winter we ice fished and used spear decoys to lure

in muskies and when they came, we jabbed them. After spearing we were supposed to let go of the spear but keep hold of rope it was on—then let the fish fight it out, then pull them in. I stuck this twenty-five-pound muskie and got so excited that I didn't let go of the pole, but fought and fought the fish until I got it up to the side of the hole. I popped so easy when I jerked, that I fell back right through the side of the flimsy tar paper fish shack. Stupidly I lay on the ice and all the Lac du Flambeau men out there laughed at me—it was the funniest thing they'd ever seen—me coming out of the side of the fish hut with a big muskie and both of us flopping all over the ice." Ed reveled in these good times, which would not have happened if he had still been drinking.

Living in Shell Lake was a good experience for Jim. He was a sophomore in the high school and played guard in football but weighed only 145 pounds—too light, and the bigger farm boys loved to get him down. He was a better basketball player on a great team that made it to the regional tournaments. There were no school size divisions then and Shell Lake had a student body of only eight hundred, yet they played well against Milwaukee teams from schools of three or four thousand students.

In the fall 1974, Ed decided to go back to the Rosebud Reservation in South Dakota. Jim did not want to move because he was playing on this outstanding basketball team in his junior year and they were going to the state tournament. He stayed with a teammate's family while Ed and the rest of the family had moved to Ring Thunder on the Rosebud. But they drove back to Wisconsin for the tournament and to see all the old friends they had made while living there.

Jim's team was so-so and Ed didn't think they would win, "but they surprised everyone and won the first game. We hadn't bought tickets for the second game because we didn't think they'd make it. It was a twenty below zero night and we had to stand in an outdoor line. Everybody laughed and pointed and teased us about the kind of support we gave our team. They got beat, but it was a thrill to watch them play." Later when Jim went back to his thirty-year class reunion there was a big plaque that noted that it was a legendary team because it was the first time a small school made it to the state tournament and did so well.

Ed and Carmen had made friends with Father Mark, a Catholic priest in Osceola who visited the Driving Hawks on the Rosebud. "The priest and a friend made it to Mission and asked directions to our place from some drunken winos standing on the corner." Father Mark admitted he was a bit leery of them. But he followed their directions to Ed's place way out in the country. They stopped at the barbed wire fence gate at the top of the hill and got out to figure out how to open it when Ed's son-in-law, Wayne Wilson, showed up. "He had an unbuttoned shirt on, with a bandanna tied around his head and a rifle on his back—that he used to shoot prairie dogs. Father Mark was sure he was in the real Wild West.

"Another friend, General Charles Lewis—we called him Chuck, flew his own plane to Winner where Ed picked him up to go pheasant hunting. He ran the largest cranberry marsh in Shell Lake and was president of the nationwide Cranberry Association. It was great to have these good friends visit us." Friends Ed had made when he was sober.

Jim, popular with the other students, completed his senior year at Shell Lake. He went on to the University of Wisconsin at Eu Claire and completed his bachelor's and MBA degrees at Bishop Stintz in Milwaukee.

Carmen and Ed were active volunteers in the AA program at Shell Lake. "We traveled to many towns in the area and lectured about alcohol and its effects." When they moved back to Rosebud, they helped establish an Indian alcohol program with the IHS and start a halfway house for recovering alcoholics.

Ed had made it through the Vietnam War and was successful in his personal battle with alcohol. "I believe the spirits were with me and helped me get through those alcoholic years," Ed recalls, "and I have been sober forty years as of this writing. I appreciate more than ever my dear wife, Carmen, who stuck by me through those bad times and we have been together sixty-three years. Now I truly enjoy my children and grandchildren and find joy in life because I am sober."

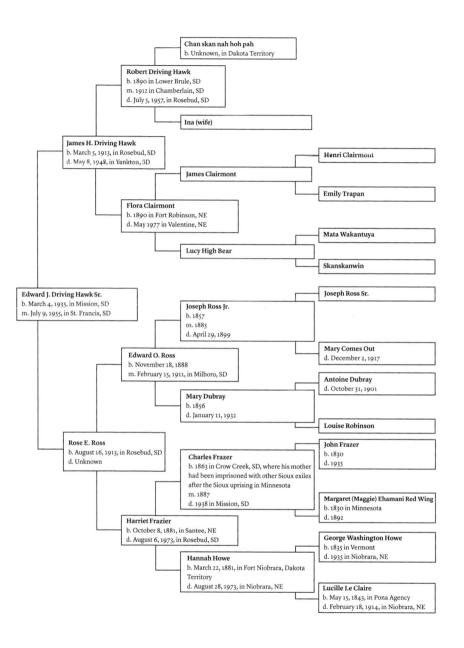

1. Ed's family tree. From Ed's collection.

2. (*opposite top*) The Rev. James Driving Hawk, Eddie, Virginia, Rose. Okreek, South Dakota, 1940. From Virginia's collection.

3. (*opposite bottom*) Sonny playing soldier with dog Fritz, Okreek, South Dakota, 1942. From Virginia's collection.

4. (*above*) Seventeen-year-old airman Edward Driving Hawk. From Ed's collection.

5. Air and ground crew of EC-121 Electronic Recon aircraft, Ton Son Nut Air Force Base. Vietnam. From Ed's collection.

6. Ed in the stable at the Ring Thunder ranch.
From Virginia's collection.

7. Carmen, Miss Rosebud, and Ed at his inauguration powwow. Mission, South Dakota. 1976. From Ed's collection.

8. Ceremony of being made a chief. Chief Fool Bear using his blood to anoint Ed chief. 1976. From Ed's collection.

9. Grandpa Edward Ross. At Rosebud Fair rodeo. 1977.
From Virginia's collection.

10. Rosebud Fair, 1977. Rose (Ed and Virginia's mother), Chief Ed, Senator Larry Pressler, Carmen, Virginia, and Vance. From Ed's collection.

11. Carmen cutting Ed's hair. She became a skilled barber doing Ed's and four children's hair. From Ed's collection.

With Love to My Family

*In quite times I think about home
and my family and how I miss you all
so very much.*

*I miss so many of the day-to-day things
we shared…. the warmth, the concern,
the easy laughter and comfortable conversations*

*Now, I realize more than ever how special you
are to me and how empty my life would be
without you.*

*That's why even though we're apart,
I feel so very close to you, my family,
for you're always right here in my heart!*

12. The poem Ed wrote while in prison. 2010. From Ed's collection.

13. Ed and Virginia in Gilbert, Arizona, 2018. From Virginia's collection.

5

Wakinyan Cangleska

ED, CARMEN, RAY, BUTCH, LORI, AND LEO MOVED TO the Rosebud Reservation in 1974 and stayed four months with Lloyd and Adele Boyd, Carmen's parents, until they got their own place. Ed asked Grandma Flora Driving Hawk if he could move a trailer to her allotment site. She agreed, but they had to get the BIA's permission. They went to the Land Office at the agency office in Rosebud. "Talked to this guy in the office and he denied the request because the lot was leased to a white rancher as grazing for his herd of cattle. They got huffy and so did I," Ed recalled. "The grass is leased, but not the ground. We can still live on it."

In the past Flora or Robert would have accepted the decision without complaint if they had even seen the land official. One time she and Robert went to the BIA office and sat all day wanting to see the superintendent about getting permission to fence the land along the road running by their home. They patiently waited, sitting through the noon hour while the superintendent went for lunch. Late in the afternoon they finally got to see the man and conducted their business in five minutes. On another occasion they had to go home and return the next day. Or if they were finally admitted, the staff acted as if their visit was an unwarranted infringement in their day. This was still the policy.

When the BIA land officer denied the request to move the trailer to Flora's land, Ed took her to the superintendent's office where the secretary told them to have a seat. After about an hour's wait, Ed stood up, took his grandmother's arm, and they strode unannounced into the office. Flora stood at the man's desk and instead of asking permission said, "I want my grandson to move onto my land! And that's how it's going to be." Ed didn't have to say a word but stood tall and menacing behind his diminutive grandmother. The superintendent asked for details and location and without argument granted the permission.

Ed recalled, "This experience really made me realize how abusive the BIA had been to the people it was supposed to serve."

The land was about eight miles from Mission. Ed and Carmen placed a twenty-four-foot trailer on a nice flat area near the creek. It was in the area where Flora's relatives the Clairmonts, Larvies, Jacksons, and Blue Thunders had their original allotments. There still were remnants of their log cabins west of the Little White River in the Ring Thunder community. But now much of that allotted land had been sold to non-Indians or leased for grazing.

The new home site was across the creek from where Robert and Flora's cabin had been and where they raised their children and where four of them died. The old dirt base of the house was still visible near a seep well they had used for water. The area was rich with wild grapes, sweet wild plums, choke cherries, and buffalo berries. Carmen made jelly from the plentiful fruit and the rest of the harvest was dried in the traditional way Sioux women preserved the fruit.

The house at Ring Thunder had neither electricity nor running water, just as Ed had known as a boy, but they made it a happy home in a green lush valley along the creek. Ed dug a four-foot-deep seep well down by the barn, which was okay to drink, but highly alkali and foul in taste so they hauled drinking water from town. Their herd of horses grazed the lush grass along the creek and Ed heard them whinnying and went to see what was wrong. A horse was thrashing about in the soggy ground. Ed and the boys roped him and pulled him out. "It was tough work pulling the horse out of there and when we finally did, we discovered a freshwater spring flowing in the muck the horse had stepped in. If the horse hadn't got bogged down, we would never have known the spring was there. It's cold and tasty water rising from the Oglala Aquifer. We built a spring box and around the spring and channeled the flow through a pipe from which we filled our buckets. Later we got it piped to the house."

There was no electricity until Ed paid the Rural Electrical Association $1,500 to erect power poles from the highway to the ranch. Many summer evenings, they sat around a fire in the yard with friends Jim Recker and family who lived nearby. Carmen's brother Bob Boyd and his family often visited, enjoying the warm summer evening drinking coffee, chatting, and laughing in sociable companionship. "It was a bit of heaven," Ed recalled.

In Wisconsin they had gotten interested in raising and breeding English setter hunting dogs and now had more room for kennels and training area. Son Leo soon became the best trainer. They enjoyed living in the country and were happily content with the dogs, but soon realized that the new business could not compete with other established groups in the area. Ed recalled, "Even with my retirement pay we didn't have much cash. One of us had to go to work."

Carmen had not been too keen about moving back to the reservation, she knew that there were many problems with poverty, alcohol, education, and crime and she worried about how her children would adjust—they were Lakota children but had never lived on the reservation. Her parents had worked at the Rosebud boarding school and their family had never been a part of the local Indian community, so reservation life was new to her. There weren't and still are not too many employment opportunities on the Rosebud, but Carmen was easily hired as a counselor at the Todd County High School, where she enjoyed working with the teens.

Ed assumed the operation of a used car lot that Carmen's brother, Sonny Boyd, had run for a couple of years. The business owed more money than its inventory was worth, so Ed contacted Dick Ham, president of the bank in Kilgore, Nebraska, to finance the operation. Ed traveled to Denver and Omaha and learned to bid at car auctions to build inventory for his business. He bought eight cars at a time, hauled them back to Mission, and hired a relative, Dick Blue Thunder, who had been to an auto mechanic school and was skilled in repairing and detailing the cars to run on the reservation roads. The business took off—they could not get the cars in fast enough. Ed brought home sixteen cars and they were sold before they were unloaded. The business took untraditional down payments such as TLE certificates or land sale options and was successful because there were no other auto dealers on the reservation. Soon Ed ventured out into trailer house sales to welfare recipients, for which the state would make the payments, and Ed financed them through the local bank. The business did well.

Ed still had $14,000 in the air force credit union and withdrew it to buy thirty-five head of cows and one bull to run on a quarter section of land. He hired help, supervised by Poncho Long Dog, to build a forty-two-square-foot barn with stalls and a corral. "We had fine time being cowboys and then we went into horse racing."

Ed's longtime friend Teddy Rouillard said he knew where he could buy a fast quarter horse for only $900 and asked if Ed wanted to go in with him to race in Pierre. "I thought that would be a good investment and gave him $450. But it didn't turn out too good—the horse couldn't run a lick, but that was my start in the racing business. I paid $6,000 for Lucky Moore, a quarter horse stud, to run the All-American futurity two-year-old races in Denver, the richest quarter horse race in the United States.

Ed bought mares from Oklahoma and Kansas and bred them

to the stud. "We raced him all that summer to get him up to triple A status, which had a ratio of one hundred or more, which was good for his breeding purposes. Then he branched out to thoroughbreds that ran in Omaha and Grand Island, Nebraska, Pennsylvania, and New York. He hired a local trainer, John Bradley from White River, who raced at those sites. Lucky Moore was rated a triple A and was raced for three years and no other horse could catch for 360 miles, no further than that. With speed index of 110 as an outstanding breeder. He bred all Ed's mares and Andy Larvie raised them on land just north of Driving Hawk's.

Another horse, My John Dear, a two-year, ran in a futurity, but he ran erratically so Ed brought him home for retraining and then performed well enough to win the South Dakota Derby. A lady from Wyoming bought him as a stud for her mares.

Ed's businesses were successful, Carmen like her job, and the children were gradually adjusting to the ranch and reservation life, but they did not like Todd County School. It was a public school, but with majority Indian students. There was no need for boarding schools now nor the boys' home at Hare School because now buses transported children from all over the reservation. It was a culture shock to the Driving Hawk children and found that they were well ahead of their peers in academic skills.

Lori hated it. Ed and Carmen felt badly that their only daughter was so frustrated and unhappy. They consulted with church members and family who told them about Saint Martin's Academy, a Catholic boarding school runs by nuns in Rapid City. She transferred and was treated kindly and she soon made friends and enjoyed her classes. The tuition was expensive, but it was well worth it to have her content.

During the summer she was permitted to drive the car during the day but had to come home when it got dark. One night she did not meet her curfew, and Ed took the pickup and drove to Mission, Rosebud, and White River but did not find her. "I called the tribal police and put out an all call and found out that she had gone to Pine Ridge, picked up a girlfriend, and driven to Eagle Butte on the Cheyenne River Reservation. Another friend joined them as they continued to Rapid City where she contacted other friends, had a hamburger before driving home on the same route—a four-hundred-plus-mile trip. All the while she was gone, the Rosebud tribal police was in contact with Pine Ridge and Cheyenne River Reservation officers who monitored her movements and notified Ed to her location. They would have intervened if there was any sign of trouble and she and her friends were safely monitored even though they didn't know it. Ed and Carmen were relieved when she returned home at dawn, but severely reprimanded her and forbade use of the car for a week.

Lori and a girlfriend enjoyed riding horseback among the hills and bluffs of the Rosebud country. As they rode, they saw something glittering and waving on a high butte. They rode to the top and saw wooden stakes with feathers tied to them, which fluttered in the breeze. There were stone pipes and small cloth bags holding tobacco arranged in a circle on the ground. The girls each took a feather and hung them in their rooms. Lori suddenly awakened during the night to noisy banging and thumping about the room. She turned on the light but saw nothing. Terrified, she moved to the living room. Her friend experienced the same frightful clamor and concluded that the feather was trying to get back to the butte. The next morning, they raced their horses to return the feathers. They later learned that the butte was a sacred site where ceremonial items were kept.

On that summer at home she met and fell in love with Wayne Wilson, a good-looking boy from Mission. She returned to Todd County for her senior year and after graduation they were married. They enrolled at Southern State College at Springfield, where Ed had gone, and took secretarial business classes. Wayne tried a general course but didn't like it and quit. They moved back to Mission where Lori was a secretary for the Rosebud Sioux Tribes' Legal Aid department, but Wayne was unemployed. Lori had children, Tomi, Kristina, and Jeremy by Wayne, but it was a troubled marriage and even though she tried to make it work, it ended in divorce.

Son Butch began as a sophomore at Todd County, but had a tough time adapting. His class work was repetitious, way behind what he had in Osceola. He played football in his junior year but blew out his knee and had to have surgery to repair the injury. That knocked him out of football, but he was able to play basketball. He was popular with most of the kids, but some gave him a hard time because he was smart, good looking, and a fine athlete. In 1978, when he was eighteen, he ran for governor. Many teenagers all over the state supported him and worked all the county fairs to get the required signatures for him to be on the ballot. Bill Janklow, Republican, was governor at the time. At the state Democratic convention Butch made a speech about how Indian kids were abused and other racial inequalities in South Dakota. Democratic Party leaders made a deal with Butch to include his concerns in their platform if he withdrew and threw his support to the Roger McKelleps, the Democratic candidate, which he did.

Butch was so unhappy at Todd County that he left and joined a friend in the high school at Gordon, Nebraska, from where he went on to graduate. He went to South Dakota State in Brookings on a football scholarship, but on the first day of practice he blew out his knee again and this time, after two operations, he could no longer play.

Ray also went to Todd County and the school created a program just for him, as there were no Special Education classes back then. He played football, wrestled, and was a good athlete. Ed and Carmen enjoyed attending his wrestling tournaments, to watch how he would get down, and set, and no matter how his opponent managed to get on top he could not move Ray, who was so big. He played defense at football and the coach told him, "Your job is to get the quarterback no matter what." Ray chased after the quarterback and tackled him even though he had already passed the ball. It was a joy watching him play football.

After graduation, Ray attended school in Rapid City for disabled students where he learned to live on his own. At first, he lived at the Workshop, then rented a place at the Jacksons', one of Carmen's friends. One night some younger men were drinking and began letting air out of tires—Ray stayed out of it but watched what the others were doing. Some called the police and Ray was arrested with the perpetrators. The police called Ed, who contacted attorney Dennis Hill who got Ray released from jail.

Ray made friends at Workshop and he and four buddies moved into an apartment where they cooked their own meals, cleaned house and generally took care of themselves with only limited supervision. At school he met Leslie Lammer, originally from Eagle Butte. She was a year older. They fell in love and began living together. Ray worked as a janitor at Federal Building and at Soo San IHS hospital. Many times, he came home from work to find Leslie drunk—she sipped wine all day. He started missing work because he thought he should stay home to take care of her. Ed and Carmen decided to move them to Ring Thunder and moved a smaller trailer for them a half a mile up the hill above the ranch at Ring Thunder.

Ray was a big help on the ranch. In addition to being big and strong he learned to drive the tractor, cut hay, and drove the pickup. He's always had a weight problem, but he kept it down while helping on the ranch.

Every day Ray drove slowly up and down the hill to work on the ranch. He and Leslie liked to drive back and forth on the Ring Thunder road and listen to the radio. Ed and Carmen were going to a horse race and told Ray that he could drive the car but not on the highway. Ed alerted cousin Alma's husband, Boney Valandra, of the reservation's police force, to watch out for Ray and Leslie, and that they were not to drive on the highway. The couple decided to drive to Mission; Boney followed them with siren and lights flashing. He pulled them over and said, "I should put you in jail—you're not supposed to drive on the highway. But I won't, but you must drive straight home and never do it again." Petrified, the frightened couple agreed and drove home and never did it again.

Ray and Leslie were happy. On their first anniversary they wanted to go to Rapid City to visit friends, so Ed took them in the car, but just as they we pulled into Rapid, Leslie suddenly had a frightening convulsion. Alarmed, they rushed her to the Sioux San IHS hospital, but it did not have the needed emergency treatment, so they raced to the Rapid City Regional Hospital where she was immediately admitted. The next day they expected her to be discharged and everything would be okay, but the doctor told Ed that Leslie was an extremely sick girl. She had been taking calcium pills, which her body didn't absorb into her digestive system but were retained in her renal system and hardened her kidneys so that they could not function—she was dying. Sadly, the family took her home to Ring Thunder and she and Ray moved into Ed and Carmen's house, so they could take care of her. She was not supposed to drink a lot of water, and she was given only ice chips which did not quench her thirst. It was a difficult time. She got so thirsty that she crept out of her room, drank the forbidden water, which her body could not pass and bloated up like a balloon and was in terrible pain. It was a constant struggle to keep her functioning and several times she had to be taken to the IHS Rosebud hospital where she was hooked to an IV to stabilize her and then sent home. This happened several times in one month until finally in May, the doctor told them not to take her home—there was nothing more they could do for her. "We'll keep her comfortable here," the doctor said, and in a week she passed away in the hospital. Her funeral was at Mission and she was buried in Trinity cemetery by the graves of Ed's father James and grandparents Flora and Robert Driving Hawk. It was tough time for Ray, who wept inconsolably, questioning why Leslie had to die. Ed and Carmen kept him busy with ranch chores and took him along on a trip to Denver—trying to keep his mind on new things to help him adjust to being without Leslie. Years later when Ray was in his fifties, he asked Virginia, "Did you know Leslie?" she responded, "I only met her once." "She was pretty," Ray said. "But she had to die." "I know," Virginia said, "that was hard." "Yup," Ray said, still missing his young wife.

Ed and Carmen's youngest boy, Leo, was nine when they moved to the reservation. "He took to the ranch life like a duck to water," Ed remembered. Like his father, Leo was an outdoorsman—he loved to hunt and trap. In the spring, all the old women in Ring Thunder wanted him to shoot prairie dogs before they got too wormy to eat. They begged him to trap porcupines, so they could use the quills to decorate their leather work and told his parents what a good boy he was to help the old ones.

His older siblings were wary of the Indian lifestyle after living so long in white society, but not Leo, he took to it with zealous pleasure. He loved dancing at powwows and relished the traditional *tonega* (tripe) soup. When at a Ring Thunder powwow, the announcer called the elders and youngsters to be first to get their *tonega* soup. Leo was the first in line. Then when the singing, drumming, and dancing started he was the first to step out. One old lady said, "I didn't know your son was crippled." Ed watched their son dancing about and laughed because he hopped around as if he had a bum leg.

The boy loved riding horses, working cattle, and was good at training the dogs and enjoyed doing it day after day. Ed bought him a little black Shetland pony, not knowing it was mean and stubborn. Leo mounted it and stiffened its legs and would not move or it would start before he was on and run away. Ed got on, but it jumped and reared and bucked him off. "We had a hell of a time with that critter. But remembered that the Blue

Thunder boys broke horses so, I hauled the pony to them. 'Bring it back when its broke and I'll pay you.'"

Two weeks later the pony returned, so gentle and calm that it didn't seem like the same horse. Leo rode the pony for a couple of years then moved on to larger horses.

While in his teens, Leo was breaking and training Ed's horses and then did the same working for a white rancher. It was a fun job and the boy had spending money.

Leo went to Bad Joe Waln's rodeo school and one day Waln called Ed. "You gotta get over here. Your son is crazy!" Leo was riding every bronc that Joe ran out. "He'd get off one or get bucked off and hop on the next. He was good," Ed proudly recalled. He competed in high school rodeos all over the state riding broncs and bulls and his parents attended every event. Luckily, he was never hurt.

Leo was an excellent dog trainer as well as taming wild critters and brought a raccoon and a skunk into the house. He removed the scent glands from a skunk—a smelly job reminding Ed of when he trapped with Grandpa Ross. The skunk was like a pet cat in the house. Virginia and family stopped by and walked into the house (the door was never locked) and after seeing the skunk waited in the car until Ed and Carmen got home.

He had no trouble with school classes and was as athletic like his brothers and played football, basketball, was in track and wrestling at Todd County. His sister, Lori, drove back and forth to school and he rode with her, but sometimes she forgot him and he had to walk the eight miles home. He and his girlfriend, Lori, got married right after high school graduation and he joined the air force with basic training at Lackland AFB, San Antonio—same place Ed was in 1952. He liked the military life and trained dogs in the canine corps. Then he was sent to the Philippines for a two-year tour and Ed and Carmen paid for Lori's way there, so she could be with him. Out of the service the couple moved to Arizona, attended Arizona State University, and then worked as a deputy sheriff in Maricopa county.

"Ring Thunder" is the English translation of *Wakinyan Cangleska*, a Lakota chief to first settle in the area. The community is a part of the *Sicangu Oyate*, Rosebud Sioux tribe, recognized by United States government as a sovereign nation. The word *sicangu* translates as "Burnt Thigh," so named after a preservation event when the band fled a prairie fire, and many had burns up to their thighs. "Rosebud" refers to the abundance of wild roses in the area. The *Sicangu* settled here in 1889 after the U.S. government divided the Great Sioux Reservation into seven South Dakota reservations. That was the same year South Dakota became a state. The Great Sioux Reservation originally covered all land west of the Missouri River in South Dakota, part of northern Nebraska, and eastern Montana. All of Todd County is Rosebud Reservation land, but once four areas in adjacent counties had been part of the reservation. It was Ed's boyhood home and he wanted to his children to know it.

The Driving Hawks became active in the community and participated in the annual Ring Thunder powwow held the last week in June. "We attended the powwow committee planning meeting when a young man, son of Oliver Moore, asked to borrow money to sell Indian jewelry at the Rosebud Fair. He claimed to be from Ring Thunder and asked for $100 and said he would pay it back after the fair, but he never did." Ed also recalled that the same guy asked to borrow one of the powwow grounds outhouses for a gathering at his place. He took it, but never brought it back. The committee wanted to arrest him for stealing, but he returned the outhouse and was never seen again.

The annual powwow was an important event in the community's life and after Grandma Driving Hawk died, Ed and family hosted a memorial in her honor at the event. "We gave away horses, star quilts, towels, dishes, and smaller items to that all who attended got something in Grandma's honor."

At a later powwow, Ed and Carmen hosted a naming ceremony for their first grandchild, Tomi, Lori's daughter. She was called Oyate Waste Winyan, "Woman Who Feeds Many," a prophetic title for how as an adult she came to adopt two nieces and a nephew after her sister could no longer care for them. The three plus her own three sons in her house made for many feedings.

At the powwow, after Ed became tribal chairman, Harley and Louie Blue Thunder and medicine man Bill Shwagman made Ed a chief. Ed recalled, "Chief Fool Bull from Pine Ridge took his blood and put it on my forehead, transferring his chief's power to me."

At the same ceremony, Louie and Harry Blue Thunder further honored Ed by naming him Wakinyan Cangleska, chief Ring Thunder's Lakota name. "I was surprised and humbled that they thought I was worthy to have that brave man's name." The chief had fought at the Battle of the Little Big Horn and afterward, even in defeat, proudly led his band to the reservation.

Then Ed's Okreek friends and some relatives on the reservation came to him and suggested that he think about running for chairman of the Rosebud Sioux tribe. As a boy on the reservation, he did not even know about tribal politics, but now upon his return, he observed how badly the BIA and current tribal government treated an ordinary Indian person. The BIA controlled the Indians' lives—one even had to get permission from the superintendent to legally leave the reservation and although it was no longer strictly followed except if the man in charge didn't like a person, then he cited the old law. No previous administration or individuals ever challenged the BIA's power. Even Grandma Driving Hawk thought it was okay when the superintendent told Indians what to do. She and others meekly accepted that's the way it was supposed to be; a hundred-year-old policy had become a way of life. Ed decided to run.

The governing body of the Rosebud Sioux tribe was made

up of the chairman, vice president, secretary, treasurer, and twenty council members, one each from districts or community throughout the reservation. These elected positions made up the Rosebud Sioux Tribal Council, whose purpose was to negotiate with federal, state, and local authorities on matters concerning the tribe; to acquire and oversee property for use by the tribe; advise the U.S. Secretary of the Interior on congressional matters and bills affecting the tribe. The council could also levy taxes and conduct trade; pass and enforce laws for public safety; and foster cultural celebration and preservation of the Lakota Sioux *Oyate* (people). Any enrolled member of the tribe was welcome to attend the council meetings, which were held the second Wednesday and Tuesday of every month and the last Wednesday of every month.

Ed pondered the idea, discussed it with Carmen, friends, and relatives, before he decided to run for the Tribal Chair position. He knew it would be a tough job but felt that he could guide the tribe in dealing with policies to address vital issues of water rights and federal and state jurisdiction. Another concern was the Black Hills settlement. This historic matter has been ongoing since the Fort Laramie Treaty of 1868 when the U.S. government promised that the Great Sioux Reservation, including the Black Hills, would be set aside for the tribes' use—to forever live in that land. They believe the Black Hills land is sacred—the tall peaks are close to the Great Spirit. Crazy Horse, the great Lakota war chief, fought to protect it from the miners who desecrated the sacred land and it is where the holy man, Black Elk, had his world vision. The United States Supreme Court ruled that the tribes were entitled to financial award for the taking of the Black Hills, but to this day the tribes have refused it; they want a return of the land.

Ed knew if he were chairman he had to deal with these challenges within the structure of tribal government, but he willing to give it his best shot. Then "Aunt Alice Dog Eyes came to see me. She was one of those old Indian ladies who could tell what was going to happen in the future. She said I would win the election and be in office two times. I respected her and the other elders who practiced the old ways and so, I believed her. I also had learned how to deal with people through my sociology major in college and I knew how to delegate authority in my military training. All this helped me administer the various departments of the tribal government."

Campaigning for tribal office was much any like political campaign in the United States, but Ed's visit to the local districts or communities usually was accompanied by a meal or "feed," as it was called. He had to pay for all of this, of course, but was lucky in having female relatives who managed the cooking, although a lot of the chore fell on Carmen.

He won by fifty votes which was challenged by the incumbent, Bob Burnette, who took the case to court. Ed needed a lawyer and his brother-in-law Sonny Boyd suggested Dennis Hill. "Dennis represented me well enough so that the court ruled in my favor." Burnette, whose own first chairman election was controversial, then appealed to the United States District Court, which also ruled in Ed's favor, and he took office as soon as he returned to the reservation.

The inauguration ceremony was on Saturday, February 14, 1976, and Edward James Driving Hawk became chairman of the Rosebud Sioux Tribe. South Dakota governor Richard Kneip spoke kind words and Dr. Ben Reifel, one of the honored elders of the tribe and South Dakota's first Indian congressman, urged the people to participate in their government. Ed and Carmen hosted a dinner and a powwow for the whole reservation and when Ed spoke, he said, "I am glad to represent the Lakota people, but I ask you to help me do and obtain what is right and just. I will represent the Rosebud Sioux tribe and I will be bound by what the people say."

His first term was from 1975–1977; Narcisse Brave was the vice president; the secretary was John King, Jr., and Phillip Amiotte was treasurer. Leo Menard was the sergeant at arms.

During the campaign, Ed had often been teased, "I suppose you'll have us all march around and saluting," referring to his military career. The first day Ed walked into the tribal office, the janitors were all lined up stiffly holding their mops and brooms, as if they were rifles, and stood at attention ready for inspection. It was all in fun, but the Indian people respected him as a veteran, because being a soldier was still important to a warrior society, but others said he was a mean old sergeant and sometimes he had to be.

In August 1977 Virginia and her husband, Vance, made a trip to Norway, from where Vance's grandparents had emigrated in the 1870s. His family had kept in touch with relatives in Opdal and welcomed the couple to "Snevegaard" (Snevefarm), which was still worked by Vance's third cousins. Europeans have always been interested in American Indians and the Opdal kin were no exception. The children were especially fascinated by photos Virginia had brought of the Rosebud powwow with the dancers in colorful regalia. In Oslo they visited Trgve Holst, who had attended South Dakota State University when Vance was there. On the morning of August 13, 1977, they were getting ready to go to the airport to catch their flight home, when Trgve called the hotel and told Vance to get that day's issue of the *AftenPosten*. Vance jokingly said, "Okay, but I can't read it." They got the paper at the airport and found the Rosebud Reservation featured in a four-page spread titled "Vi ar fra tap til tap" ("we go from loss to loss"). There was a large spread of reservation places and photos of powwow drummers, a sweat lodge, an old man by his dilapidated trailer home near abandoned autos. There was a story about Narcisse and Agnes Sharp Fish and photos in their little house and another of Crow Dog making a traditional item. There was a picture and story of Ed Driving Hawk as tribal chairman. The article discussed the culture, lack of employment, and other challenges faced by the chairman and the tribe. Virginia and Vance were amazed at the coverage in that Nordic land.

As tribal chair Ed dealt with many individuals who had complaints against the BIA, TLE, and IHS and he often felt overwhelmed and helpless with how little he could do. Joblessness and poverty were the norm—even though he established some small tribal businesses to address this plight—people came to his office to ask for clothes or shoes for their children so they could go to school, or for assistance in getting government surplus "commodity" food. In addition, he often adjudicated private individual family concerns.

He was in office only two days, trying to orient himself to his duties, office procedure and practice, when an elderly couple came to see him. They were very respectful to him, shook his hand, but they spoke only Lakota, so Ed had Farrell Dillion, his *misun* ("my brother" in the traditional way) and a friend from Okreek, as the interpreter.

The elders told that their forty-year-old grandson visited when they got their Social Security check and forced them to sign it. Then he cashed it, kept most of it, leaving very little for their needs. They wanted Ed to scold him or do something to him that would stop him from taking their money. Ed told them to bring the grandson with them and they all came in the next day. He had consulted with Farrell about what to do and the advice was, "Scare him."

The grandparents with their grandson entered Ed's office. Ed asked the elders to wait outside and when they left, Ed recalled, "I put on my air force sergeant's face and glared at the grandson. 'What's this about, taking your grandparents' checks and cashing them?' "

He was a good looking well-built young man, whom Farrell investigated and found that this able-bodied grandson had never done much work and liked his wine. "I thought they owed me something for staying with them and taking care of them," was his excuse.

"Do you have a job? Do you have any income? Do you pay rent?"

"No," he said.

"Now, this is between you and me [even though Farrell was in the corner]. If you ever bother your grandparents like this again—take their money, I'm going to call the police and have them bring you to my office. I am going to shut the door and kick the shit ought of you. Do you understand?"

He turned pale and trembled as he heard Farrell interpret my threat. "No," he quavered, "I won't do it again."

"I told him to apologize to the elders when they came into the room." Farrell translated, "Grandma and Grandpa, I am sorry, and I will never do it again."

"They smiled at me and shook my hand as if I were the greatest person on the rez. They never came back to complain and so as far as I knew, the grandson never took their money again. In fact, he was seen cutting wood for his grandparents and truly helping them, as he should have done in the first place."

This incident was one example of the elder abuse that was occurring on the reservation. The reservation system corrupted traditional Lakota culture; in the old days, children and grandchildren respected, fed, and cared for their elders until they died.

Another time Ed gave Harry Blue Thunder, in his seventies, a job cleaning the community hall. His grandson came and complained, "How come this old man has a job when he gets Social Security. I don't have a job—can't get one and I have no money."

"All right," Ed said, "come up to the office and I'll give you a job. We need help cleaning the tribal fair grounds and getting things ready for the fair."

He never showed up and Harry kept his job.

After Ed was in office for a few months, he found that there was little accountability of monies that came to the tribe. He and treasurer Phillip Amiotte decided change had to be made and a good start would be with the annual Rosebud Fair. The event began soon after the reservation was established and was held on the fourth weekend in August. It was originally like many non-Indian county fairs where vegetables, fruits, etcetera, were harvested, judged, and awarded ribbons—all to encourage the once nomadic Lakota to farm. A powwow was traditionally held with money awards in the various dance categories. Later a rodeo, carnival, and musical night entertainment were added.

Tickets were sold for the powwow and the rodeo, but when Ed studied the past records of the fair, the rodeo always lost money. Ed's administration suspected the ticket sellers held back some of the funds. Treasure Amiotte distributed a certain number of tickets to each seller and after they sold the tickets, he would collect the money then give them more tickets. In this way, he knew exactly how much cash he should get. The sellers were mad as hell that they had to account for money. In the past, they took a little off the top before turning in the funds.

There were some national stars lined up for the night shows: Buck Owens, Bill Smith, and Ronnie Millsap. Again, Phillip set up a system that all tickets and monies were accounted for, and the fair made money—the first time it ever had. However, it cost Ed politically because of the bitter ticket sellers and their families, who resented losing their side money.

Ed recalled, "Phillip was good with numbers and kept good accounts—probably for the first time in tribal government. But he believed in star signs, astrology, and read his horoscope every day. One time he read that it was an inauspicious time and that he should not get out of bed. So, I had to send clerk to his house with the payroll checks to be signed."

Ed was talked into riding a cow at the rodeo—the people wanted to see their chairman bucked off. It wasn't as easy as the calves he rode as a boy in Okreek, but he climbed into the chute like as if it were a bull instead of a fat cow. The gates opened, the cow jumped out, and two cowboys, one on each side, came out with pillows to catch Ed when he fell. The cow hopped, Ed was bucked off, but missed pillows and hit the ground hard. The crowd roared! Grandpa Ross was in the stands and he laughed until he cried. "The bumps and bruises I got were worth it," Ed said, "to see Grandpa enjoying it so much." It was hard to get grass to grow on the hard-packed dirt powwow grounds, so the council hired a company from Hot Springs, South Dakota, to sod the place. The fee was $6,000, but Ed figured it was needed for a nice spot for the dancers. The new sod had to be frequently watered to keep the new grass green and growing. When the powwow opened with the grand entry and all the dancers moved in time to the drums and the Lakota song. As the dancers stomped in, little green frogs began to jump out of the grass and into the spectator stands. Old ladies screamed, men yelled, and kids chased the frogs. It was a mad turmoil for about an hour until all the frogs were out of the grass.

The first fair during Ed's administration was successful and the second year was even better. People came from the all over the reservation, and it was often "family reunion" time for Indians who no longer lived on the reservation. One year, Senator Larry Pressler, running for reelection, came and Ed, Carmen, Virginia, and Vance posed for a picture with him. Another year, after the tribe had a voter registration drive, Tom Daschle came to plead for native support in his run for Congress.

The fairgrounds sat idle for most of the year and when a local minister asked if they could be used for a revival meeting, the council allowed it. "The minister was really happy that they were going to have an Indian minister to speak. I was surprised to find out it was my cousin Ralph Powless. His mother was Alma, Mom's sister who had died from burns she got from an exploding gas stove. Ralph and his wife and kids had come through Rosebud and came down to see us. Naturally we put them up—they were family. He was a born-again Christian and preacher. It was fine for a week, then it was two weeks—Carmen was getting tired of feeding them, doing their wash while they just sat around, prayed, and drank coffee. They had no money, that I could tell, and when asked how he supported his family, Ralph said, 'God will provide.' After another week, I asked him if $200 would be enough provision to leave. He took it and left. Somehow, he convinced the local minister to hold the revival and of course, he was the money given during offering.

"Then a group of traditional followers wanted to hold a Sun Dance at the fairgrounds, since Christians had a revival there. So, we had to say yes. A guy came to my office and said you better come see what's happening at the fairgrounds. I went out there and in the middle of that $6,000 green grass, men were digging a big deep hole for the Sun Dance Tree. We told them they had to put it all back the way it was after their doings, but they never did."

Ed respected the traditionalists, who were often full bloods, and who followed as best they could the ways of their ancestors. There was no militant confrontation on the Rosebud as there had been at Wounded Knee and on the Pine Ridge Reservation in 1973. The elderly at Pine Ridge accused chairman Dick Wilson of nepotism, corruption, and abuse of the elderly and traditionalists. The Oglala Sioux Civil Rights Organization (OSCRO) was formed to impeach Wilson. That did not happen as Wilson resisted by using armed guards, the Guardians of the Oglala Nation (GOONs), to intimidate OSCRO members. OSCRO held a meeting and invited member of the American Indian Movement (AIM) to defend the Oglala. On February 27, 1973, three hundred armed Oglala Lakota and AIM activists went to Wounded Knee and declared it a liberated area. They occupied the church and blocked roads. Two hundred FBI agents, federal marshals, and BIA police surrounded the site. Leonard Crow Dog, chief and spiritual leader, led ceremonies to prepare for battle. Many people from many tribes came to Wounded Knee to support the Ogalala through this protest, which lasted seventy-one days and received intense national and international media coverage.[1]

The site of Wounded Knee had special significance to the Lakota as being the site of the massacre of three hundred of Chief Big Foot's band who had camped there on the way to Pine Ridge after fleeing the Standing Rock area.[2]

Ed had known Russell Means, one of the AIM leaders, and his brother Ted from Hare School. The Means boys were urban Indians who had lived in Cleveland but were sent to Hare School to be exposed to native culture as they attended school in Mission. Shortly after he was in office, Ed and the tribal council passed a resolution supporting AIM at Wounded Knee. But Chief Crow Dog and War Bonnet, a Rosebud tribal member, and others were imprisoned. The National Council of Churches raised $415,000 for Crow Dog's defense and Vine Deloria Jr. was one of his attorneys.[3] Ed and the council petitioned South Dakota governor Richard Kneip to urge the release the men on Ed's assurance that he would be responsible for their good behavior and conduct when freed.

"I had great respect for Crow Dog, he stood up for what he believed in even though he went to prison. I was grateful that he supported me in tribal issues."

Ed realized that the tribe needed raise their own cattle to not be so dependent on buying beef at exorbitant prices. Ed introduced the topic at a council meeting and some of the districts questioned who knew enough to run such an operation. But Ed told them that there were successful Lakota ranchers on the reservation who would guide the project. The council set aside two thousand acres of land and appointed successful Indian ranchers Bob Waln, Ollie Wright, Dick Whipple, Opie Lapointe, and Martin Luther Jones, a white rancher married to an Indian woman, to oversee the operation. They hired a manager and borrowed money from the American Indian Bank in Washington to buy one thousand head of steers, one thousand head of heifers, and a thousand cows, and bulls to service them. Cattle prices were down when they bought, but at the end of the year, prices were up, and they sold the steers, paid off the loan, and the ranch was free and clear. They kept one thousand heifers and cows that they bred and sold as breed cattle. They also had steers and it was a successful operation. Four years later when Ed went out of office the new chairman, Norman Wilson, sold the cattle to white supporters from Pierre who bought them for little or nothing and they turned around and pastured them on the tribal ranch.

Another innovative project Ed led was for the tribe to establish its own mortuary and burial insurance, which provided a coffin and assisted with a wake and the funeral. Off reservation, burial services were expensive and funeral directors were often ignorant of cultural traditions, but now when someone died the body would have local care. Robert Burnette, the former tribal chairman, still bitter about being defeated by Ed, often complained to BIA authorities in Washington DC of misdeeds he suspected Ed of doing. Now he accused Ed of nepotism, using tribal funds to employ relatives, getting a kickback from the mortuary business. The funeral home the tribe used was in Valentine, Nebraska, a few miles south of the Rosebud Reservation border. Ed got a call at two o'clock in the morning from the county sheriff in Valentine reporting that the hearse was parked on the Main Street with a body in it while the mortician was in a bar. Ed arranged for someone to get the hearse and deliver the body to the mortuary, then fired the mortician. Burnette filed a complaint and within two weeks, civil rights people came from Washington and said, "We finally got you, Mr. Driving Hawk, we know you fired Don Luxnor from the mortuary for political reasons."

Ed did not argue with them and told them to go ahead and investigate and asked them to leave his office. Two days later they came back and sheepishly said, "Why didn't you tell us the reason you fired him." "I said, 'You didn't give me a chance, you came in here to raise cane with me because I fired a guy who was in a bar. You should get your facts straight before making accusations.'"

Another venture Ed instigated was the Lakota Products pottery project, which made four to five thousand pieces a week and provided employment for several Indians. The employees worked under an unorthodox program plan—on "Indian time," which meant that if a thing was to be done, or event happened it did not necessarily follow regular twenty-four-hour clock time. The pottery workers came in day or night, whenever they were available, and there was no trouble keeping orders, which came from local businesses and tourist centers in the Black Hills, filled. Another tribal enterprise employed local seamstresses who sewed lovely ribbon shirts and skirts favored by young Indians to wear at special occasions such as high school or college graduation.

Ed had always enjoyed hunting, but the reservation land did not have a large pheasant population for the sport. So, the tribe set up a program setting so many pheasants per quarter section of land aside for hunting. The pheasants came from the South Dakota Fish, Game, and Parks Department, which also supplied grouse. "Governor Janklow was pretty damn mad about that, but it made for good hunting for a while. The next administration didn't keep it up though."

As chairman, Ed encouraged the BIA to hire qualified Indians for government jobs. George Keller, a tribal member, became superintendent of the BIA office in Rosebud. He was a social worker for the BIA and knew how the system worked and did his job okay, but his personal morals were his downfall. He was superintendent for three or four months when George's secretary, a timid woman—more like a teenage girl—from Okreek, went to see Ed. She entered the office with her head down and hands clasped tightly together, clearly frightened, and spoke so softly, Ed barely heard her say, "George makes passes at me and says I have to go to bed with him if I want to keep my job."

Ed called George into his office and sternly and loudly

reprimanded him for abusing the woman and moved her to another job.

Later, another woman, Ann—married to the chief of police—made a sexual harassment claim against George to the BIA and investigators came from headquarters in Aberdeen. She had asked for a short-term loan and Keller told her that if she went to bed with him, she'd get it. However, she refused and turned him in. Ed told the BIA about the incident with the Okreek girl and they transferred George to San Carlos Apache tribe in the middle of nowhere.

Ed didn't have much luck in personnel he hired for the tribe's education department, which administered BIA funding to the reservation schools. First, he hired Chuck Ross who, had a PhD in education, but he lasted only a month and left without any explanation. Joe Marshall took the job next, but he also took off without giving any notice. Norman Knox, of Okreek, stayed in the position, but didn't accomplish much; he like to attend national meetings and get a per diem for his travel.

The issue of land on reservations was complex, but more so after, it was broken up into individual parcels or allotments under the Dawes Act of 1887 and held in trust for twenty-five years. After that the feds issued individual patents in fee simple, which allowed the land sale if the owner so wished. This was part of the federal government's assimilation policy intended for each Indian to own land.[4]

After the original owner died, the land was divided among the heirs and became fractionated among hundreds of descendants. The Indian Land Consolidation Act of 1983 ruled that when an Indian died, and he owned a fractional share of trust land, that share would go to the tribe.

Many tribal members were unaware of the law and unknowingly lost their land. It was not until 1966 that the issue was resolved with the 1996 Cobell Indian Trust Settlement Act. The act, named for Eloise Cobell, the treasurer of the Blackfoot tribe in Montana, filed a lawsuit in behalf of up to five hundred thousand plaintiffs. She had found mismanagement in the government's administration of trust lands. Her lawsuit showed over a hundred years of discrepancies in accounting for the income from leases or payment to the tribes and individual members. The settlement set aside $1.5 billion administration settlements paid to individual, $60 million for higher education and $1.9 million to tribal governments to purchase fractionated shares. This allowed tribes to consolidated shares into commonly held land. The federal government had messed up, but the Cobell settlement benefited the tribes.[5]

Both Virginia and Ed sold their fractionated shares inherited from their parents to the Rosebud tribe and that from Grandpa Driving Hawk from the Lower Brule Sioux tribe.

A long-established project on reservations was the Tribal Land Enterprise program (TLE) started in 1943. It gave the authority to buy and sell land for the tribe using certificates of interest. According to Rosebud's web site its purpose was to consolidate reservation land and the program allowed individuals to exchange their trust land and interests for certificates, which could be redeemed for cash or land assignments. This was meant to help individuals to exchange small scattered acres for more consolidated areas on which one could make a living. Under the TLE program the tribe could buy land and individuals could negotiate with the tribe rather than several individual sellers. But unfortunately, there were abuses of the system by self-serving tribe and BIA officials under previous chair and council administrations. TLE had been buying land for many years, but the certificates issued in return were often worth less than the air value of the land. In Ed's administration the person in charge of the BIA land department came to Ed and said he has suspicions that a former chairman and his cohort had received eighteen quarters of land in exchange for TLE certificates. Each certificate was worth about $7,000 a quarter, but the individual seller never received anything for them. The chairman issued all the certificates to his friend.

After an investigation all the fake signed TLE certificates were found. Ed asked the BIA area director of to investigate, but the person who made the complaint changed his mind and did not want to testify.

One of the major problems that existed on the Rosebud and other reservations was the amount of Indian land going out of trust status. During Ed's term in office, there were about 240,000 acres of reservation land offered for sale by individual allottees. The tribe did not have the funds to purchase these lands. The estimated value of the land was $26 million. Ed had the council's approval to write directly to President Gerald Ford, bypassing the BIA, which we knew would take forever to respond to our request. We asked for a loan of $5 million to purchase these lands and asked for $3.6 million to buy outstanding TLE certificates. But it was a negative response and no monies were loaned.

Rosebud country was dry land with little productive farmland. Ed persuaded the council to apply for a grant from the U.S. Department of Agriculture for an irrigation project of $3 million for an irrigation project for eighteen thousand acres. He was unaware that when the tribe drilled that other the wells had an instrument that monitored the level of the Ogalala Aquifer and that there were federal laws governing its use. If the aquifer shrunk more than 20 percent, the entire downstream wells would have to shut down their irrigation. However, neither our tribal council nor Ed knew of this restriction. In addition, the local white ranchers worried that because the tribal project was monitored, they might have to shut down their irrigation projects. They contacted the former chairman noted above, whose sidekick viciously went after Ed, accusing him of fraud, criminal negligence, and other baseless accusations to get him out of office.

Ed didn't realize how badly someone wanted him out until one evening after work he stopped the car at the top of the driveway at Ring Thunder, got out of the car, and as walked over to open the gate—when *ping*—a rifle shot struck the pickup. He hit the dirt—military training kicking in, and crawled to the other side of the pickup, managed to get his rifle from the pickup and took a shot at a person silhouetted up on the hill. Whoever it was turned and left. Ed called the police in Mellette County, which was off the reservation, but they did not come. He believed the dispute over the water rights caused the shooting and now believes that the elders of his vision had protected him that day and in other times of danger, "Even if I hadn't had the vision until years later."

Ed was honored to be elected as chairman of the United Sioux Tribes of South Dakota in October 1978. The group was a nonprofit entity organized to develop and assist the Indian people in the eleven South Dakota reservations. They met once a month in Pierre, South Dakota's capitol, and dealt with problems that concerned the whole area.[6]

In October 1977, Ed became chairman of the National Congress of American Indians (NCAI)—a united voice for all the tribes of the United States. A national organization that represents the views of Indian tribes in the United State and to protect the tribes from those who wished to destroy reservation lands. Based in Washington DC, it kept an eye on legislation that affected the tribes and was also a lobbying group for tribal issues. It began in the 1950s and dealt with the termination policy of the U.S. government. It could be a powerful force but was dependent on tribal groups for its financial support.

As tribal chair and head of the NCAI, Ed often went to DC to meet with congressional representatives and South Dakota's senator, George McGovern, told him, "I don't know why you Indians expect Congress to work for you when none of the Indians ever vote. If they voted, we would be encouraged to do things." Ed returned home and through United Sioux Tribes and the National Congress of American Indians, began a national voter registration drive for the American Indians. It took off like fire. On the Rosebud only 10 percent of the population voted, but after the registration drive and an effort to get isolated residents to the polls, 78 percent voted the next year. Most of the other reservations had similar success.

In 1980 the NCAI encouraged tribal members to register to vote and then to vote for candidates at the state and national level who were sympathetic to Indian causes. Most Indians are unaware of how effective their votes can be. Ed believed Indians had been too passive and did not act when faced with disenfranchisement. Whether it has been intentional or not, polls are inaccessible to persons who have no transportation or if they do, it takes all day to get there. There has been gerrymandering in setting electoral districts in South Dakota that divided reservations so that they cannot have an effective bloc of votes to elect Indian representation.

The NCAI convened in Albuquerque, New Mexico, and Ed's campaign manager, Cleve Neese, had everything under control. He coordinated the details of the campaign, typed Ed's speeches, and did the backstage work. The chairman of the Quinalt tribe of eastern Washington State nominated Ed and a unanimous vote elected him chairman.

In his acceptance speech, Ed thanked the congress for the honor and the crowd cheered. Off stage, the *Lakota Times* and other newspapers interviewed him and took pictures. Jubilant family members surrounded he and Carmen—they cheered, wept with joy, and embraced the newly elected chairman—it was an emotional moment. Reporters yelled questions as Ed tried to make his way to the elevator. A young man strode ahead yelling, "Make way! Make way for the chairman!" In the elevator, Ed thanked him and asked his name.

"Don't you remember me? I'm your cousin, Olive's boy, Ed Clairmont." Later Ed's kids called him "Bingo Ed" because he loved to play that game.

After a brief rest in their room, Carmen and Ed then went down to the banquet. On the way they were called to the bar—which Ed never frequented anymore. "We found many of my

Ross relatives celebrating the election; Uncle Donald and wife Willimina, cousins Chuck and Punk Ross, and Bingo Ed. Willimina sat in my lap for a picture—they were all proud of me."

During Ed's term as chair of the NCAI he and Carmen attended Jimmy Carter's inauguration, and during his term Ed was at the White House when he signed new Indian legislation. In President Reagan's administration, Ed served on the Indian Advisory Board. They also attended Gerald Ford's inauguration after Nixon resigned and both were thrilled at being at these auspicious events and were grateful to be able to do so. Ed expressed his amazement at how far he had come from being a boy in Okreek.

As leader of NCAI he found many small tribes being challenged for their water rights by big business or nearby white ranchers who knew these tribes had neither the financial funds nor knowledge to protect themselves. The NCAI cultivated Indian leaders and attorneys who specialized in water issues and they were successful in defending tribal water rights.

Ed had to deal with the FBI in his position as tribal chairman and during his term with NCAI. He thought they deliberately harassed him because of when he had to testify at the trial of two brothers who allegedly killed a drug dealer. The two owed the dealer money and when they didn't pay him, he threatened them and followed them home. He kicked in the door of the house and charged in only to be met by shotgun fire; he died at the scene. The brothers were arrested and charged with murder; but pleaded self-defense because of the threats the dealer had made. Ed had been asked to testify about the prevalence of drugs on the reservation. As part of his comments, Ed told the court that in the past ten years there had been 257 loss of life crimes that had never been investigated by the FBI. Ed believed that this was one of the reasons that there was no respect for the law on the reservation. The judge asked the FBI agent to find out if this was true about the uninvestigated cases. The next day the agent came back, said it was true, but had excuses because they didn't have the time and there was often lack of evidence to investigate the crimes. The judge said he did not want excuses, "I'll give you thirty days to give me a report as to the status of these crimes and we're going to do that until all of the crimes are off the books."

As a result, the FBI was not too happy with Ed and they came into his office and charged him with selling a business that was a mortgaged company. Ed showed it was a legal sale by producing the contract he had with the buyer and bank, which had approved the sale, so they left. However, they continued to follow Ed. "Wherever I went an agent was not too far away. One time I was on a flight, when I recognized Agent Quigley nearby, I stopped, and I gave him a copy of my itinerary while in DC—'Here's my schedule of where I'll be on this trip, so it won't be so hard for you to follow me.'" The agent insisted that he wasn't following, but Ed believed he was because of Ed's claim at the trial.

About ten years later, after Ed moved to Phoenix, he got a call from the FBI agent who said he needed to talk to him about some dinosaur bones stolen from the reservation and what he knew about it. Ed was puzzled. "I did not know what he was talking about, but later found out that he was referring to 'Sue,' the Tyrannosaurus Rex dinosaur discovered on the Cheyenne River Reservation in South Dakota." Sue Hendrickson and others from the Black Hills Institute in Hill City, South Dakota, had explored land owned by Indian rancher, Maurice Williams. Hendrickson found the dinosaur named "Sue" after Hendrickson. The Institute had William's permission to evacuate and move the bones and paid him $5,000. However, Williams claimed "Sue" was his; the Cheyenne River tribe said it belonged to them. The U.S. Department asserted it was federal property because it was on trust land. The FBI got involved because it was on reservation land. "Sue" ended up at the Field Museum in Chicago.[7]

Ed never found out why the FBI thought he knew anything about the dinosaur.

Ed also had contentious issues with Bill Janklow, who was South Dakota's governor when Ed was tribal chairman. "He was anti-Indian from the start and never said anything good about the Indians even though he represented poor clients on the Rosebud in 1966–1973. He had a brash and flamboyant way of doing things—always had to get his way. On the reservation, he had a reputation as a lady's man and rumor was, he fathered many illegitimate kids spread out over the reservation."

Janklow had been South Dakota's attorney general and was elected governor in 1973 and reelected in 1982. He was elected again in 1994 and 1998. The voters sent him to the U.S. Congress in 2002 but he had to resign after he killed a motorcyclist on a country road and was convicted of second-degree manslaughter.[8]

Ed said, "From the time I became tribal chair, Janklow and I never got along. I met with him many times over tribal issues, but the biggest was law and order reciprocity been the reservation and the state. Tribal police often had to pursue criminals but had to stop at the reservation border and vice versa for South Dakota troopers. Janklow did not agree with the need for reciprocity because he said Indian police did not have the training the state troopers had. This was not true our police trained as well or better.

"Another issue was the sales tax collected on the reservation. Non-Indians who lived on the reservation paid the South Dakota tax, as did all the Indians, but all this money went back to the state and tribe got nothing. Therefore, the tribal council passed a resolution that because non-Indians residents represented seven percent of our population, we would pay a like amount collected to the state. This seemed to us to be a fair arrangement for all concerned. We were discussing the resolution in a council meeting when I got a call from Janklow.

'Hello!' he yelled. "Who in the hell do you think you are? You are proposing a tax resolution, but you have no right to take the state's sales tax.'

"I said, 'I didn't know it was the state's tax—I assumed it was a reservation tax.'

"Janklow answered, 'As far as I'm concerned you can just go to hell!'

"'Well,' I said, 'If that's the way you feel about it, Governor, you can go to hell too!' I hung up and went back in the meeting and told the council that the governor questioned the jurisdiction of the resolution, but I recommended that we pass it with the understandings that we'd pay 7 percent of the collected money to the state—whether they wanted it or not. The governor called me again. 'I changed my mind; I aim to support you on this sales tax,' and hung up." So the Rosebud Sioux tribe first reservation in South Dakota to develop a sales tax program.

"It was also the first time a governor told a tribal chairman to go to hell, and the chairman told the governor to go to hell. Over the years, our relationship was such that Janklow would have nothing to do with me and I would have nothing to do with him. He would ask for a meeting, I would cancel, or he did the same. This went on for the four years I was in office. When I ran for reelection the governor supported my opposition and he urged tribal members to oppose me."

The governor apparently remained antagonistic to Ed, which led to other harassment.

Ed had traded in a car for a newer model and the new owner of the trade in was driving on the highway when he saw flashing lights in the rearview mirror and heard a siren. A South Dakota patrol car pulled him over. He rolled his window down and pulled out his driver's license as the officer said, "We got you now, Mr. Driving Hawk—you were doing seventy in a sixty-five-mile-per-hour zone."

The patrolmen did a double take at the sight of the white

man in the driver's seat. The driver said, "Sorry, I'm not Driving Hawk. I guess you must have checked the plates—he had owned this car." He showed the bill of sale and driver's license for proof, "and I don't think I was speeding." The patrolman said nothing after scanning the items and nothing more came of the incident.

In addition to the contentious relationship with the governor during Ed's term in office another controversy rose in the fall of 1979. The *New York Times* reported that millions of dollars were unaccounted for or misspent on the reservation. It was a very inaccurate report. The journalist did not know how the auditing process worked. The tribe hired a private firm, who then prepared a draft form of the audit, the tribe reviewed it and then auditors prepared the final document. This went to the federal government, which determined the questions on allowable costs. The *Times* reporter based his story on the first draft only and before giving the tribal council a chance to respond.[9]

Ed had other interesting experiences as tribal chair, but the extraordinary part was the respect that many Indians gave him as they would a traditional chief. As chief he had the privilege of attending many traditional ceremonies. One was the unveiling of the peace pipe that the White Buffalo Calf Woman had given to the people. The story is that two men went out to hunt near what is now Pipestone, Minnesota. A beautiful young woman stood before them; one man was afraid, but the other lusted after the woman. He reached for her and a dark cloud came, thunder boomed, and when all cleared, he was a skeleton on the ground. The woman told the other man not to be afraid because she came from the Buffalo People to bring a sacred bundle to the people. He ran to the camp and a large council tepee was erected and all waited for the woman. She unwrapped the bundle and held a red pipe before them. She told them how to use it in seven ceremonies and said, "Use the pipe for peace, never war." She left and walked to the east. As she went, she became a white buffalo calf.

This pipe and its tradition had been with the Lakota for thousands of years and it was kept and cared for by generations of the same family who displayed and smoked it in a special ceremony attended tribal leaders. This happened in one-hundred-year cycles and Ed was in office when the centennial event happened. Arvol Looking Horse was the pipe keeper and the ceremony was held at his place on the Cheyenne River Reservation. Ten Lakota men walked into a weathered old shed behind Arvol's house and were invited to sit on the floor around an old trunk covered with a buffalo hide. Looking Horse slowly and carefully removed the hide, opened the trunk and lifted out a leather bundle, held it to the men before he carefully unwrapped the pipe. He put it together, tamped in tobacco, lit it and offered it to the four directions, the sky and earth. He passed it to the seated men who prayed before they smoked and thought good thoughts for the Lakota people. After all men had smoked, Looking Horse tamped the ashes out of the pipe, dismantled it, rewrapped it, and put it back in the trunk. As far as Ed knows, it is still there and will be opened again in 2076. Ed said, "I felt extremely humble and honored to be part of this traditional ceremony."

Ed recalled told how Grandpa Ross attended a Yuwipi ceremony to find a lost person and as tribal chairman Ed attend several similar ceremonies. A distant relative, Robert Steed, was a medicine man who led Yuwipi ceremonies. He was born to a family that had many children and they could not feed another one—there being no commodities or Social Security back then—Lucy and Jim High Bear Clairmont, Grandma Flora Driving Hawk's parents, raised Robert. He took the name Clairmont and attended boarding school with Ed's dad. James became an Episcopal priest, and Robert took the name Steed again, trained under an old medicine man, and became a highly respected one himself. He was an uncomplicated man, with little knowledge of the outside world. One day he came to visit and chatted with Grandma Driving Hawk while we had coffee. Grandma said, "Robert was supposed to be our son, but he didn't want to be—so he left us, but he is like a son."

Ed's good friends were brothers Harry and Louie the Blue Thunder. In their youth they had been rowdy, carousing young men, but they quit drinking and settled down to work in the Ring Thunder community. They invited Ed to a "sweat," which was held in a large domed tent or "lodge" of willow poles covered with canvass. The tent was airtight to keep the heat in during the ceremony. "The medicine man, Robert Steed, crawled into the tent and I and a few others sat in a circle. Outside of the tent was a hot fire where rocks were heated. Young boys carried in hot rocks on long forked sticks, placed them in the center, and Robert poured water over them and clouds of rolling steam surrounded us. It was so hot it was hard to breathe, and the sweat ran off like water. Robert called the spirits to come and to listen to our prayers for help and protection for ourselves and our families. We sang, thanked the Great Spirit, and crawled out of the lodge. I was wringing wet and relieved to be out where I could breathe. This ceremony is not for one with a weak heart or breathing problems because it is physically taxing. It is the traditional Lakota way of sacrificing oneself during the hardship of the sweat lodge for the good of others. We believe it is the lodge of the Great Spirit."

Ed participated in a peyote ceremony of the Native American Church. "In this ceremony, peyote, a little button-like thing, was eaten as a medicine, but also to promote visions for the user. It had been banned by the U.S. government until the 1960s when the Native American Church was recognized and thus fell under a Constitutional right. Many people, including Christians and DEA officials, did not approve of these ceremonies because peyote caused the user to go into a trance; it was a hallucinogen.[10]

"This ceremony," Ed recalled, "was at Spring Creek with fifteen people sitting on the floor of the room. The peyote leader spoke and then the lights went out. It was totally dark, but I saw sparks flying around the room. The lights came on and I saw some items had moved to different places in the room. The leader said he was going to tie himself up, but a spirit would untie him. An assistant wrapped him in a blanket covering his head and his whole body and tied with knotted ropes. The lights went out and again there were sparks flying about the room. The lights came on and there he stood—untied— the blankets and rope were on the floor. I never did figure out how he did that.

"The leader told me that he would send a spirit to protect me in the form of a doe. It was one or two in the morning when I got home and pulled into our driveway. About halfway down the road I saw a doe standing in the middle of the road.

"At another ceremony, we ate puppy soup. It was not bad tasting, but after I saw a small puppy in the soup—I had trouble eating it. I remembered the pups I saved when I was a little boy at Ponca Creek. Robert Steed conducted the ritual for a feeble woman who had cancer. The same thing happened: lights went out, sparks flew, but now the people sang and sang in Lakota. The lights came on and Robert blessed everyone by waving sacred smoke about the whole room. He prayed to the spirits to help her; he sat down, and the lights went on and chanting filled the room. When the lights came back, he asked her if she felt anything. She said she felt something passing over her—that could have been Robert moving—I do not know. Before the ceremony, she was too weak to sit up, but now she sat in a chair, spoke, smiled, and obviously felt better. She had been near death, but she was healthy and happy when she left.

"In the small community of Ideal, my cousin Darlene Eagle Feather asked Grass Rope, another medicine man, to hold a ceremony to heal her sick child. Grass Rope was known to have phenomenal healing powers and was highly respected on the reservation. He followed the same procedure; the lights went out, sparks flew. This time when the lights came on, we chatted and laughed, ate puppy and other soups, and had cakes and pies—everyone was happy. The next part of the ceremony was to ask the spirits to protect me while I was running for office. Grass Rope sang and prayed while helpers wrapped him from head to toe in a tightly tied blanket. The light went out and I could see nothing, but heard singing, and felt feathers touching all over my body. When the light came on, there was Grass Rope standing free of his bindings. He said to me, '*Tahanshi* [cousin], I'm sending a large bird to carry your spirit, to protect and be with you.'

"I went home and told Carmen who, was in the back bedroom, what had happened in the ceremony as I sat at a table in the living room. Suddenly there was a *Boom Boom Boom* and the front door flew open. I stood up alarmed, stepped back and heard wings flapping as if a bird was flying about the room. It flew twice around and then it quit, and the door slammed shut. Carmen heard it and felt the air move as the bird flew about the room. I cannot even try to explain what happened, but I believe Grass Robe sent a spirit bird to my home.

"A few days later, Raymond and I were in the north pasture driving around near a peaked butte and there was this large golden eagle perched on a dead tree. It flew right at the windshield with wings three or four feet on either side of the pickup. 'What was that?' I cried. 'I don't know, Dad, but let's go home.'

"After that, we often saw bald eagles roosting on a tree across the creek. One was especially large as it perched and looked like an old man with a blanket over him. I think my elders' spirits were part of this protection and I needed it, after someone took a shot at me. My relatives persuaded me to run again, but when I began campaigning for a third term, the reservation politics turned nasty and dangerous. My opponent, Norman Wilson, won by fifty votes but I did not contest it—I was tired and ready to give it up."

During Ed's first term, he had helped George Keller be

appointed as BIA superintendent of the Rosebud Agency. "But he forgot that I had helped him and in my reelection campaign, he supported Norman Wilson, who won the election. Afterwards, they both came to the office and asked me if I intended to stay until the end of January as the tribe's constitution read or leave on November 1. I said, 'I'm not married to this job, so I'm ready to go whenever you want.' So, a couple of days later, Wilson was sworn in."

Ed bitterly recalled that, "Keller turned on me after I was out of office. I was pasturing cattle with Bob Carr's herd; he was a neighbor and non-Indian. During the summer I'd run my cattle on his land and in the winter, he would run on my range, which had more shelter. It was more cattle than the reservation unit should carry, but with the combination of Carr's land and mine, there was more than enough acreage. I was walking down the street in Mission when Keller and Wilson came up to me. 'We're going to fine you for over grazing and cancel your range unit.'

" 'I don't know what the hell you think you're doing,' I said and explained how Bob and I worked together and had more than enough range. However, they canceled the range permit and now that I was no longer in office, I had no influence in any matter and without any grazing land, I was out of the ranching business."

Ed has no regrets about his time on the reservation and being tribal chairman. "It was an interesting, educational, and challenging experience, but when my term ended, I was glad to be out of all the underhanded politics and factional conflicts that besieged me as chairman."

6

Too Strong to Be Broken

IN DECEMBER 1973, ED AND CARMEN AND FACED another geographic and cultural relocation almost as great as moving from the Wisconsin woodlands to the Dakota plains of the Rosebud Reservation. Now they had to adjust to an urban population in the sprawling metropolis filling the desert valley of Phoenix, Arizona. In South Dakota their nearest neighbors were Lakota three miles away. Now a few yards separated neighbors of Hispanic, Caucasian, and Asian backgrounds. The landscape was dominated by white spires of Mormon temples near crowded housing developments and shopping malls. The quiet ambiance of the isolated ranch was replaced by a continuous roar of auto, truck, and bus traffic. Glaring light pollution obscured the night stars and moon. But they adapted.

They rented a large two-story house with a small grassy front yard, a rock garden in the back where they soon learned to watch for scorpions. A compensation for the noise, crowds, and lack of privacy was a swimming pool, which all enjoyed and was necessary as exercise as there was no demanding ranch chores to keep them in fit.

Ray moved with them and was thrilled to have a large room of his own and his personal television set with many channels as opposed to the three in Dakota. Daughter Lori, recently divorced, also resided in the big house with her three children, who loved the pool.

"We could no longer make a living on the ranch without grazing land and we wanted to get away from the nasty reservation politics," Ed recalled. Politics on Indian reservations has been described a bucket of crabs; one will start to crawl up, sometimes almost makes it to the top, when the ones left behind pull it down. No matter what innovative policies were established by the current administration, they were undermined by individuals who did not think they benefited from the program.

Ed felt rebuffed and hurt not to be reelected. "But after pondering the pluses and minuses of reservation life, Carmen and I decided it was for the best. As I look back, I think I was beginning to feel the effects of that damn Agent Orange; I just didn't feel very strong and even though Ray was a big help, ranch work was physically taxing without the other boys at home. Plus, the cold and snow of Dakota winter was tougher to bear."

After military hardship and reservation turmoil he now became an entrepreneur. "I had my military retirement and was financially secure enough to start a business."

Ed and Jim, Butch, and Leo formed E. Driving Hawk Construction Company, a road construction company, the only Indian contractors in the Southwest, and proceeded to bid on reservations projects, which gave preference to Native American–owned businesses.[1] They were awarded the projects but had to negotiate the price of each job. As part of each agreement they supplied 10 percent of the cost, which was done by leasing trucks to haul gravel and other material needed for the project. They also provided their own workforce. "So, the truck leases, plus office supply expenses and crew payroll, made up our required ten percent. We had an arrangement with the finance department of the Mormon Church to provide all the funds for building bridges and bonds and cash for payroll. It worked well for all concerned.

"It was all within the legal procedure to work with the tribes, and we had big jobs in Colorado and all over the Southwest and we made a lot of money. We did all the roads on the Salt River Reservation north of Phoenix and on the Gila Reservation south of Phoenix and a nineteen-mile road on the T'odo Odom Reservation down by Sells, Arizona.

Ed had a contract with the Mohave tribe where his business had a controlling interest in six casino sites along the Mohave river. "I paid the tribe $147,000, earnest money, and four of the sites were to be sold. We also had an agreement with the Trane Company to install a large air-conditioning unit to supply AC to the tribe's casinos plus supplying water and sewer. The casinos would then pay Trane for use of the system

"Each of the casino sites sold for $15 million to the Chippewa tribe of Oklahoma, Bill Laughlin of Laughlin, Nevada, and the Santee Sioux tribe. We met with the tribes and the four companies involved in the purchase, which was also approved by the BIA.

"I ventured out on my own with an IHS job at Elko, Nevada, to remove the asbestos from the hospital and rebuild the houses all around there. The job was for $500,000 and I hired two engineers to design the job and son Butch was the overseer. We completed it on time, within budget, and made ourselves $125,000. I also hired a bondsman who managed the bonding process on the jobs. I thought I'd go back to South Dakota if I made enough money to restock the ranch in South Dakota, but decided to stay if the jobs continued, and it would be hard to give up our backyard swimming pool.

"We had an excess of cash and I found out that IHS needed someone to supply eyeglasses for Indian children in the area, so I set up Wakaya Wambli, Eagle Vision, an eyeglass shop right across from the IHS hospital in Phoenix. That was successful because IHS guaranteed payment, we gave good products for the Indian children, and gave them a choice of frames. IHS paid us thirty-four dollars for each pair of glasses and we made twenty-five dollars profit. The previous non-Indian providers had not given such good service. IHS was pleased. We expanded the program to take in the Luke Air Force Base, the army base at Fort Wahchuka and one in Oklahoma, which was very profitable because of their large personnel.

"In all we had seven shops."

All was going well with the business and Ed's family until one day he had excruciating pain, was rushed to the ER, and it was found that he had cancer in his right kidney. "It really laid me low, in agony—physically and emotionally drained."

It was during surgery to remove the cancerous kidney that he had the vision of his elders in that warm, bright, safe place where he could not stay. He awoke in the hospital to Carmen holding his hand. "I was glad to see her but felt an aching longing for something—not sure what, until I remembered seeing Dad, Grandpa Ross, and the others and I knew they would always be there for me."

Ed was physically weak, in pain and impatient with his recovery from the surgery and hospitalization. Then Jim, who had been helping him, went to work for the IHS, and Ed could not manage the business by myself, so he closed the eyeglass programs, later realized it would have been a good income for the family even if he had to hire someone to run the business. "I had no energy—I was too weak and sick—all because of that damn Agent Orange, but I am proud that Jim stayed with IHS and is now the director of the Great Plains area, which includes South Dakota." His daughter Lori also made a career of working for IHS from which she is now retired.

Ed recalled after he had more strength after that, "John Adams, from Illinois, came to see me. I had met with him at an NCAI meeting and he suggested the possibility of forming an American Indian bank to administer tribal funds. Adams told me that he had a graduate degree in banking from the University of Tennessee and had been a banker. We found out that it was legal for tribes to issue their own banking licenses and if we established a national bank strictly for tribal funds, they would no longer be dependent on the federal government's control of their money."

In his time as Rosebud Tribal Chair and his term with NCAI, Ed learned about the status of tribal funds and how they were often mismanaged by U.S. government entities—especially the BIA. The Sioux tribes alone had over $250 billion for settlement from the Black Hills and Missouri River tribes, had funds also held in trust by the U.S. government. The tribe did not have control over its own funds.

Senator George McGovern recalled how 138 families of the Missouri River tribes received meagre compensation for the 21,497 acres they had to abandon to the damn waters.

Senator George McGovern recalled the event in his foreword to *Dammed Indians Revisited*:

> As a freshman member of the United States House of Representatives, I sponsored bills in 1958 that would have provided settlement to the Crow Creek and Lower Brule tribes for the reservation land and resources for the Fort Randall Dam project. However, the compensation requested in these bills was nowhere near the tribes' original asking price.
>
> Neither the tribes nor individuals received adequate compensation the land and resources; and the BIA in Washington inefficiently administered the monies they did get.[2]

Ed knew about that land confiscation because of Grandpa Driving Hawk, an enrolled member of the Lower Brule tribe, whose allotted land was a fertile patch along the Missouri River, which was flooded after the Missouri River dams were built. He died before the compensation was awarded and so his heirs, Grandma Flora, Virginia, and Ed got the settlement of $400 each even though the land was worth much more.

The two tribes had no control over what happened to the settlement funds, as did many other tribes in the United States even though they were considered sovereign nations. Now Ed found out that these nations could issue licenses with the same legal procedures of any state or county. If a tribe did not have laws covering an issue, the federal law would prevail. This knowledge led him to be receptive to John Adams's proposal for establishing the United States Reservation Bank and Trust (USRBT), which they did in 1999. Ed owned 51 percent and Adams 49 percent of the USRBT. Then Ed obtained a license from the Rosebud Sioux tribe for operating a federal institution or a bank and a license from the Santee Sioux tribe and one from the Maricopa Indian community at Sun Lake, Arizona, to operate a bank on their reservations.

Ed explained how this was done. "Before any tribal government deposited funds in USRBT, it published a legal notice in local newspapers to alert all tribal members of this intent. Tribal government or individuals deposited funds in the bank, and New York Life Insurance Company guaranteed all our deposits and they passed them over to their investment house. We in turn had the USRBT guarantee interest rates of two percent to the investor and one percent to the insurance company, which left us with two percent for us. We were operating within the law.

"My son Leo had retired from the Maricopa sheriff's department, and he became one of the vice presidents of the bank and helped me set up headquarters in a building at Scottsdale in the Maricopa Indian community. We rented large rooms and opened our accounts at Bank of America.

"USRBT was making a good amount on deposits and New York Life was satisfied with it. We made money and were able to buy nice clothes, a car, and Carmen and I went on an Alaskan cruise. It was fun to see more of Alaska—the land and water—much different from flying over it." Ed also shared his wealth with family members, including buying new car for his mother, Rose, and stepfather, Lawrence Posey; gifting his half brother, Arthur Posey's, daughters with a car, and sister, Virginia, with money. He also helped with college funds for his grandchildren.

All seemed to be going well until John Adams, a vice president of USBRT, without Ed's knowledge, moved funds into a Swiss bank—where it remains today. Then he took another $3 million for his own use and deposited it in Grand Cayman Island. "When I found out," Ed sadly recalled, "I stopped his ability to tap into the accounts and fired him."

Without Adams, the bank still prospered until "I got a call from Bank of America that another one of our vice presidents had attempted to transfer $20 million from our joint account to his private one, but they alerted me before the transfer. I had not approved of the move and they stopped it. The Security and Exchange Commission learned of this attempted transaction and put a hold on all our accounts. The United States attorney confiscated it all and charged me with violating a section of the SEC code.

"At about this same time, my health was failing because of the Agent Orange exposure in Vietnam. I was taking as many as thirty pain pills a day—was forgetful and acting goofy from the medicine. I fought the charges for eight years with a court-appointed attorney. I had no money because the court had seized $22 million of USRBT's assets. I don't think that lawyer was interested in trying to prove me innocent—all he did was delay court hearings and negotiate a settlement. But sick as I was, I fought until I was exhausted—worn out and too feeble to fight anymore and I was in big trouble.

"The SEC accused us of bilking our investors of over $70 million between March 2000 and February 2001. I told the judge that I didn't know what John Adams was doing until he deposited money in a Swiss bank. The judge said I should have known what was happening. I may have suspected something, but my health had really declined and then I had a stroke in May 2001, but the judge did not think that was an excuse for my ignorance. Adams used me, as an Indian man, to set up a banking system for the tribes as a cover for his bilking operation. I made sure that the bank met all tribal legal requirements and that New York Life insured all deposits to protect investors, but it was all a cover for Adams's illegal activities.

I was too good hearted and naively trusted him, but Adams conned me good, left me to face the music and a year in prison."

Weary and disheartened Ed finally agreed to plead guilty to wire fraud and in turn, he would get a year's probations. "We went to court. The judge said, 'I want you to stand up and tell us all the wrongs you have done?' "

Ed rose from his wheelchair and declared, "I have not done anything wrong, everything I did was legal under tribal law. The money was guaranteed. No money was stolen."

"The judge said, 'If you don't know what you did wrong, I'm going to give you one year in a federal penitentiary in California—so that you can figure out what you did wrong.'

"I said, 'I'll be there a year, but will still say I did nothing wrong.'

"My bull headedness cost me a year in the Western Division Federal Prison Hospital in New Port, California. I was concerned about what might happen in prison. I'd always heard about how dangerous it was, filled with hardboiled crooks, for whom crime was an accepted part of their lives. I worried how cruel these inmates would be, but I was not afraid. I felt that my ancestors' spirits were with me and I'd survive this time just as I did two wars."

The Federal Correctional Institution on Terminal Island, California, is located at the entrance to Los Angeles Harbor. It was once a receiving station and barracks for court-martialed prisoners. When Ed was there, it was a medical and psychiatric institution and he served his time in the hospital because of his illnesses and having to use a wheelchair. More notorious people than Ed served time here; big timers like Salvatore Bonanno, Al Capone, Timothy Leary, and Charles Manson.[3]

The day came when Ed had to report to Terminal Island on July 8, 2009. He didn't get much sleep the night before and Carmen didn't have to wake him up. He rose, had his shower, dressed, had a cup of coffee, but didn't eat breakfast. "My stomach was in knots. I rolled myself out of the house and managed to keep my chin up as Carmen and I got into the back seat of Lori's car. Her husband, Juan, was driving. It has tough time—I was worn down physically and emotionally weary and sick to my stomach. I held up on that long drive but was glad when we stopped at a motel to stay the night before I had to report the next day. That night Carmen and I held each other, loved, and wept. I told her how she had always been the steadying core of my life and how much I appreciated her support through all the trying times I'd put her through. She agreed that we had been through a lot, but we had made it despite the hardships. I assured her that we'd overcome this separation and I'd survive prison."

Carmen walked by Ed as Juan pushed the wheelchair and shook Ed's hand when he had to leave him at the prison gate. Lori hugged him, weeping as she walked away. Ed and Carmen clung to each other, tears mingling in a last kiss. A guard opened the gate and Ed wheeled himself into the prison. "Oh Lord, it was so hard to go away from her and hear the gate shut behind me. I followed a guard into the admission room, did paperwork to make sure I was the right person being admitted. Thee guard told me to stand and as I struggled to my feet one of two big black women held me up while the other searched every part of my body—even my anus. But I didn't flinch—being naked didn't bother me—not after being so at Hare School and in the service."

It was the beginning of a life that stripped him of most of his identity. His clothes, shoes, ring, watch were all taken away. He steeled himself as the admission procedure continued, rules and regulations explained, until he was finally led to a single room in the prison's hospital. Exhausted, Ed pulled himself up onto the hard bed and wept himself to sleep.

The monotony began, but Ed adjusted "I knew about institutional schedules such as eating, going to bed, and rising at a set time every day. It was much like life at Hare School and the service. But not having a choice of what to wear, being under constant surveillance, and having to get permission to do anything or go anywhere in the facility was rough. The most difficult aspect was the loneliness—I missed Carmen and my family so much it was near unbearable."

Ed kept a diary of his time in prison and Virginia saved the letters he wrote her in which he told of his exile from his family and how soon a support group found him.

"I was apprehensive about prison life after hearing negative stories about gangs in there and sometimes physical and sexual abuse, but two days after I checked in, I got a message from an organization of Indian inmates who wanted to meet with me. The floor nurse gave me permission to go out to the yard with other men for exercise and free time. One of the Indians pushed me out to meet the twelve other Indian inmates. They, many Sioux, an Oneida from New York, and a several Navajos and Hopis, greeted me. One of the Navajos said he had met me when I was NCAI chair. He respected me as an elder and took me under his wing, helping me with the wheelchair and pushed me about to go play cards or just visit."

This gathering of tribal men was not unusual because Ed had experienced such bonding in basic training and in Korea and Vietnam. "White guys often called us 'Wahoo' and would dance around like they thought Indians did. We Indians put up with it and were there for each other and the group in prison was the same. They gave me a radio to help relieve the boredom of sitting in my room. I believe the Indian spirits of our ancestors guided us to support each other."

In June 2009 Ed wrote Virginia, "So here I sit for a year and a day and hope the sentence will be cut to seven or eight months if not shorter. I have been in worst places and survived, so I will do it again. I am just sorry I had to put my family through this, but I hope everyone understands that I did nothing wrong.

"I am in the hospital section of the prison—my meds are brought to me and I don't have to go to the mess hall because they bring me my food (which is bad). Tell Vance the C rations were better than this food.

"The inmates do all the cleaning, bed making, etcetera. I am still in a wheelchair and need meds twenty-four hours for my pain. All in all, the medical care is okay, not much to be done for me other than give me my pain pills—I'm just lonesome.

"The young inmates treat me really well. They do all there is do for me—make my bed, change, sheets, clean the room, get me ice or water or anything I need. I am their old Grandpa, [he was seventy-four], most of them probably never had one. Many just want to talk about home and family and I listen to them. It helps the time go by.

"I have read six books since I've been here. I'm currently reading *Lonesome Dove*—a good read. Every day is about the same here.

"I bought an insulated cup and batteries on the black market. The currency is postage stamps. They're used for gambling in card games, betting on football, etcetera.

"The nurse told me I was spoiled because I had a snack at night—guess she doesn't understand about diabetics needing to keep our sugar up.

"Carmen, Lori, and Juan are coming over on the 3rd. It will be good to see them, but I will be lonesome when they leave. I got a nice letter from Arthur [Ed's stepbrother] in California. I appreciated it."

Ed looked forward to getting mail because otherwise every day was the same, but after he hadn't had any from Carmen or Virginia, he asked the nurse to check and she came back with nine letters. Ed was delighted but upset that they hadn't reached him sooner. "I do not know what the hang up was, but it was torture not to hear from home."

On Christmas Ed wrote, "Mrs. B. played the violin for us and read the Christmas story from the Bible. It was great," but the sound made him think of Grandpa Ross and he felt a sharp pang—he still missed the old man. Then he thought of Rose, his mother. He hadn't wanted her to know he was in prison and would write her a letter then have Carmen mail it from home. When Rose called Carmen and asked to speak to Ed, Carmen said he was in the hospital, but was doing okay. Ed had been in and out of hospitals so frequently, his mother didn't question this excuse. Rose asked Virginia if she had heard from Ed and truthfully said, yes, but did not say where he was. But neither Ed nor Virginia knew that their stepfather, Larry Posey, had somehow found out about Ed. Years after Larry's and Rose's deaths Virginia helped clean out their garage, opened a drawer of the workbench, and found news clippings of Ed's trial and prison sentence. He had never told Rose or ever discussed it with Virginia.

Ed was able to call Carmen on her birthday, January 15. "Jim and the boys are taking her out to dinner. I hope she has a good time. I sure miss her. I will be with her next year. I told her to have chicken fried steak when I get home.

"Another time I called her but had to try five times before I got through. Then we got cut off, and it was too late for me to call again. It is frustrating, because we were only allowed to call persons on an approved list and in a limited time frame. Our home phone was disconnected and I had to call Carmen's cell phone. I needed her to send me fifty dollars and when I didn't get it, I wrote an angry letter to her—I was really upset and complained about it. But then, this thirty-year-old orderly, a black guy, heard and gave me a stern lecture on how our folks at home are keeping things going and that it is hard on them. He made me feel guilty and sorry, so I tore up a letter to Carmen in which I took all my ill will out on her. This inmate was well educated and been there for seven or eight years and had one and a half left to go but had a good outlook on life. I wish I could adopt it. Carmen did send fifty dollars and I called to apologize to her. I was glad to talk to my kids when I could and especially to Carmen. I miss her so much—can't wait to hold her, kiss and hug her again. I love her just as much or maybe more than I did as a young man. I wrote a poem about missing my family."

Ed managed to adapt to his confining existence and though he still often felt bitter and frustrated as to the reason he was penned up, he didn't let it depress him, he was still "sunny" to his roommates and the prison staff.

"January 17, Mrs. B. had Bible study today. It is good to pass the time and gives me strength. Some of the staff and inmates don't like that she's doing this, but that's their problem.

Reading the Bible here made me remember when Grandma Driving Hawk made me read it—all those "thees" and "thous." I wish I had taken it seriously then.

"January 21, no drink, no food, and no meds after midnight as I was scheduled for an ultrasound on my stomach and guts to find out if I'm bleeding inside. I was one hurting Indian before they took me down at 0930 for the fifteen-minute procedure. I sure was hurting until I got my meds. I am anemic and now have an iron pill added to my daily drugs.

"I had a nasal congestion attack and had trouble breathing, I asked for a decongestive, but the pharmacy does not have it. I used stamps to buy some through the black market. I am having a fight with a Nurse Williams. She forgot my nerve pain pill at 0600, but she said it was my error because I am senile; I may be getting there, but not yet. Another nurse gave me it to me at 0800."

"My first encounter with the nurse, Ms. W., was the first of June. I had flulike nausea and diarrhea at around 2300. I rang for the nurse and she slammed open the door and proceeded to holler and chew me out for ringing the bell. She reminded me that this was a prison.

"I had a lot of pain in June and July, neuropathy in hands. One night I was in such pain, I cried and yelled with the pain. Dr. Dag, the prison doctor, authorized Percocet when I needed it. I called the other nurse and she bought the pills. However, with Ms. W. I rang, but she never brought the pills. I told the doctor and he had me moved from isolation room 209 to 201, where there were other inmates.

"Every night shift that Ms. W. was on (1900–0700), she came in at 0400, violently shook my bunk to wake me up, to pierce my finger for blood (test for blood sugar). All the other nurses let me take my own test when I wake up between 0430 and 0530.

"Ms. W. also comes up with some complaint, 'Mr. Hawk, your chair is in the wrong place. Mr. Hawk, you ran the water too long. Mr. Hawk, turn your light off, it is no heat lamp' (it was). After I turned the lamp off, she turned on the overhead light. On four occasions, she failed to deliver my narcotic pills for my pain—80 mg Vicodin, 40 mg Oxycodone, 5mg Percocet.

"I called for the pills and she said, 'I gave them to you. You were asleep, and I woke you to give them to you.'

"I decided to stay awake to check her out. I called when it was pill time, but she never brought the pills, but claimed that I had been asleep when she gave them to me.

"Another time, I woke at 2330 and waited until 0100 and called for the pills. Again, she said, I already gave them to you.

"When she did deliver my pills, she walked in, banged the pills down without a word, went out the door and slammed it shut.

"Because the nurse said I was forgetting that she gave me the pills, I was sent to the psychiatrist who gave me a series of tests to see if I had memory loss. There was nothing wrong with my memory. Now I started to keep a log of when I was to get the pills. The log showed that I was not getting my pills on time.

"Later, Ms. W. came into my room, 'I understand you have a complaint against me, that I never give you your pills. I might have been late, but I always gave them to you. I thought Ms. Lopez was the one that never gave you the pills. I guess the administration will be talking to me, thanks to you.' I did not say anything to her. Later I found out that Ms. W. was selling the pills she was supposed to give me."

On January 29 Ed wrote, "I woke up this a.m. with pain so bad, I could barely get out of bed. I got some hot water from the sink for the coffee pot, but I spilled it all over the floor. I jumped out of the way so as not to burn my leg. Really hurt. My roommate cleaned it up for me. The next day, the pain was terrible, I tried to sleep all I could—no exercise.

"I set up a regular work out schedule of thirty mines twice a day for three days and one day off. It was tough on my flabby body and especially my legs, but it got better as I got stronger. I lost twenty-five pounds and can do forty sit-ups and twenty push-ups—which is great because I did zero when I first came here.

"On January 31, I woke up and thought it was Monday. My roommates teased me, but I lost a whole day. So just for fun and to pass the time, I made a calendar of the time I had left to serve. The pain was not as bad. I did my exercises. Something was going on—the boss man was asking questions. There were some narcotics were missing. Ms. W., the night duty nurse, had finally been caught.

"Ms. W. was some mean witch. One day I went to make a telephone call, but the phone was turned off. She said it would be back on at 2050 and I had to wait until then. That was when we were let out of our cells. When I did get on the phone, she told me I had to hang up because there was no opening. I'll go by the rules even though it seems like I'm the only one that does.

"In addition to pills and other nursing care, the nurses had to take a black rubber hammer and pound on all the windows and glass doors to make sure none were loose so that an inmate could not escape. The windows also have two-inch iron bars vertically placed with glass on one side."

Ed was moved from his lonely room to one he shared with two roommates. Of course, he had no choice in selecting them and recalled, "Some were okay, others were not, but they were all interesting characters," but he managed to get along well with most of them but was thoroughly disgusted with others.

"This cell has turned into a crybaby room—my roommates complain about the doctor, the nurses, and the food. They go on for hours until they go to sleep." He was glad to have headphones for his radio so "I don't have to listen to them and their foul mouths. They use the "f" word in very sentence. When I was in Vietnam, the troops cussed like that and I started to pick up the language myself. I made a conscious effort not to do it.

"They also started going on about sex—how they had it and even with penguins—can you imagine? It was disgusting and showed they had no morals."

"A new inmate moved into my room. He has cancer and is on chemo. He is a redneck Jew, self-centered and vain. He would not walk by three blacks standing in the hall 'because they stank.' He does not want to be close to blacks or Mexicans; I don't know how he'll make it if he's allowed in the yard. Every thirty minutes he goes to the bathroom and does he ever stink. He walks around constantly and farts. He has two years left. He and six others set up a trust where each put up $350,000. His friend left for Europe with the funds. One of the trust holders went to the FBI and accused him and the other person of stealing. His friend died in Europe and now this bigot faces prison. He finishes chemo in three days and is supposed to go back to his room—I sure hope so.

"Byron Evans, another roommate, was an okay guy, but he had cirrhosis. It won't be long for Evans. His belly is all protruded today. He can barely move and doesn't have the strength to get out of bed.

"They took him to an outside hospital. He always talked like he didn't believe in God. Earlier one of the nurses wanted to read the Bible to him, but he said, not ready for that. When he and I talked, and I could see the fear in his eyes. When Mark, a roommate, helped him sit up, Evans clung to his arm—he was really scared. I'm sure if he believed in God he would not be scared. I've seen believers die and they had a peace about them—no fear.

"But surprise, Evans came back, he didn't die. Pneumonia made him so sick—got it from lying in bed and not moving. That was on December 9 but he eventually he died on January 30. A young inmate in his thirties came here for shoulder PT. He took care of Evans, doing whatever he could to help him—even cleaning his butt. Evans was in terrible pain and suffering the last few weeks of his life and once was revived with CPR. When he came to, he started going to Bible study. He had accepted the Lord within his last week of life. He had suffered so; it was for the best when he died. I wrote a eulogy for a memorial held for him."

Ed was usually the oldest inmate in the hospital and often served as a father figure or "grandpa" to the younger inmates. The young inmate who had helped Evans broke down in tears, mourning his friend, but also venting that he didn't think he could make it through the two years left to serve after the thirteen he already served for bank robbery. Ed listened with a sympathetic ear and encourage him to be strong and not let prison wear him down—he would make it if he tried. "I told him he had many things going for him, he was smart, had a nice personality and had grown up a lot." Ed knew he was going home soon, "So I gave him my twenty-four-hour book of scripture readings, told him how to use it and that it would help him make it through the next years. He's nice kid and I know I can get him a job with Butch in the construction company."

Ed often played cards and was good at many games. "I won the gin rummy tournament. It started out with four players in four weeks and narrowed down to two of us. I won after two days of playing. The guy I beat pouted like a baby because I beat him. I told him it was just a card game—not that big a deal, but he was still upset over losing.

Ed's next roommate was a Mexican who ate peanuts and then around 0100 he fell out of bed, scared the hell out of Ed. "His naturally dark skin turned bright red and he could not breathe. He hit his head, had a concussion, and was in and out of consciousness. We called the nurse and he was taken an outside hospital"—Ed never knew what happened to him.

Ed noted that roommates "Dan and Howard were clean freaks, each accusing the other of being dirty." Another was "some sort of a diplomat from Nigeria and in for credit card fraud and told about his travels all over the world." Another was "An elderly man in his seventies, but he acts like he's much older and has Alzheimer's. I don't think he knows where he is."

For a brief period, Ed was not the oldest inmate when a seventy-nine-year-old college professor came in. He was sentenced for money dealings with the government, but more likely for smoking dope. He told tales of traveling around with his wife in '67 VW van—a really hippie auto. He had colon cancer and was having a tough time.

"A new Indian man is here from California; he took $9,000 from a casino and is in for three years on a drug charge—he has two to go. He said he was next to Burning Breast [Sioux inmate], from Rosebud in the regular part of the prison. He's only in his twenties, a diabetic with a blister on his toe so bad that he was close to losing it.

"Doc Dag gave me steroid shot in my knee. After I got it, my knee felt good. He said after it healed, he'll do the right knee.

"I received my release date of 29 March 2010. My case worker said, she'd go for six months in a halfway house which will put the day at 28 October 2010. Sounds good!"

Ed wrote to Virginia, "I have forty-seven days left and this bump in the road will be over. I have used these eight months to build my body back up. I exercise daily and am stronger. When I get home, I'll be out of the wheelchair. One big mistake I've ever made was to use an electric wheelchair. I became feeble, lost all the strength in my legs and arms. I've regained about 60 percent back.

"An inmate from the next cell asked me to read a court paper he received; he could not read. He was about sixty years old— it's hard for to realize that there still are people who can't read.

"Our eighty-one-year-old cellmate keeps running away—he can't get off this floor but goes to other halls and rooms on the same floor.

"Then there's clean freak—if one us drops a piece of paper; he is on it before anyone else can get. If I use the can and he's there with his spray bottle to clean the seat and all around. He drives us nuts!

"I wrote a poem, 'With Love to My Family,' to show how I loved and missed them. I made my own calendar to keep track of the days and months passing—which was slow.

"I was getting stronger doing my workouts and even walked down the hall without my wheelchair. I met two inmate who had been here in the summer. The wanted to make sure I remembered them. I overheard them talking about me. 'Do you know he is the head chief of all the chiefs and Indians?'

"'I heard the Feds had to go out to get him.'

"I had bad dreams—woke up, heart pounding—I'd been reliving the war.

"I smuggled in a chocolate pie last night and was just getting to eat it when the nurse (a nice one) caught me. I said, 'It's for you, Happy Thanksgiving, I mean Happy Valentine's Day.'

'I can't take it,' she said. 'I can't eat chocolate, so go ahead and eat it.' We laughed because I said Thanksgiving instead of Valentine's Day.

"My bunkmates and an inmate from the next cell came over and we got to telling jokes, stories and laughing a lot. The nurse came over and said, "This is a prison, you're not supposed to be happy." That made us laugh even more. We are here, so we'll make the best of it.

"A bunk mate who has been in the cell with me has not showered in two weeks and he's getting rank. I hope the nurses start to smell him and say something. I finally told the nurse and she talked him into showering. It sure smells better now.

"We had powdered eggs—I like them with catsup. I leaned to like them in Korea, so they hit the spot.

"Mrs. Docett, my case worker, came by. She had only a word of encouragement, but no release date yet. She gave me a set of clothes—two shorts, two T-shirts and towels. The barber came and gave me a good haircut and we said prayers together.

"There are other 'Skins' here, a Navajo and a White Mountain Apache and some California Indians. A Northern Cheyenne and a New York Seneca who's standoffish—jealous for some reason. All in for drugs—if drugs were legalized, they could close all but one prison. We visit in the yard and it's good to talk to them and to be outdoors in the sun and away from my bunk mates, who complain all the time.

"This inmate, Kirby, is leaving tomorrow, but he's having a hard time getting ready to go. One would think he does not want to. He spent two hours looking out the window. He should catch the bus at 0730, but he has not packed. At 0645 they came to get him, the nurse told him he had ten minutes. When she came back, he was still putting things in his laundry bag, and everyone was helping him. He left wearing the same sweat suit he wore every day—even sleeping in it—it smelled. The nurse made him bathe last night, but it was too late to get new clothes so that was all he had to wear. She sprayed him with deodorant. He left, but the orderly found his glasses, ID, and other papers he needs—sure hope he gets on the bus."

At last Ed's term in prison was over and he reflected on the eight months he had served. "I wouldn't have had the sentence if I had knelt to the judge and said how bad I was and how sorry I was for all that happened. But I got up from my wheelchair and said, "I did nothing wrong. Adams and his cronies used me and took advantage me, but I made it."

"It was a lonely time—I spent so much time by myself and I missed my family. Yet a positive outcome for the year was that I got myself back into good physical and spiritual shape. Besides the exercises for my body, I went to Bible study for my soul. I read *The New International Reader's Version* subtitled *Free on the Inside*.

"I look back over the years and the bad times I had, when I was so sick, I wanted to join my elders in that bright, warm safe place. I know that they were protecting me all the time even in prison and I came out with a renewed belief and faith in God. I was both physically and spiritually strong—too strong to be broken."

Epilogue

ED WAS FREE. CARMEN, JUAN, AND LORI WERE WAIT-
ing as he was wheeled out of prison on February 23, 2010. He
had survived his sentence and was mentally and physically
stronger than when he entered the institution. The first stop
on his way home was at a restaurant where he had a good meal
of steak, baked potatoes, and pie—the best dinner since he left
home. They drove home to Phoenix where his children and
grandchildren gave him a grand welcome. He slept in his own
comfortable bed and had a loving reunion with his dear wife.
Being away from her had been the hardest part of his prison
sentence. The next day he had to move to a halfway house to
be reintegrated into society, where he stayed for one month,
his activities monitored, and received counseling on how to
live on the outside. He didn't have much to do other than lay
around and read. He was physically strong, but not mentally
or emotionally ready to tackle the world; he looked forward
to the weekends spent at home.

All went well after he was finally at home, but after about a
year he recalled, "That that damn Agent Orange attacked me
again!" For the rest of his life he will suffer from the effects of
that toxic exposure. He had blood pressure spike six years ago,
which caused a tear in his aorta and was warned that it could
rupture any time and that would be the end. His chronic pain
causes more blood pressure spikes and trips to the ER. "But,"
he disgustedly states, "I'm still here."

In 1985 he woke up paralyzed and couldn't walk. He had

many weeks of treatment and physical therapy but continues to have intense pain in his back and neuropathy in his hands and feet. He needs injections of pain killers and steroids to numb his feet and back so that he can move.

During the 1980s veterans received very little compensation for combat-related injuries and Ed credits George W. Bush for getting that raised. His father, HW, had been wounded in WWII and was getting a pittance for his combat related injury. "GW worked with Congress to up the VA disability payments."

After Ed had a cancerous kidney removed in 2011 and other health issues of heart disease and diabetes, the VA rated him as 100 percent disabled and another 100 percent disabled because his illness is combat related—all attributed to exposure to Agent Orange. His retirement income and disability pay gives the family financial stability.

"We spend a lot of time on doctors' appointments, but otherwise we don't do much," Ed says. "It's so difficult for me to go out." Carmen must load his wheelchair on the rack attached to the rear of the car and Ed is frustrated that he can't help her. They were driving down the freeway one afternoon and a car, horn honking and passenger motioning, pulled beside them. They then realized that the wheelchair had come loose and was dragging behind them; they were able to rescue it, but it was damaged. Fortunately, the VA supplied a new one.

Carmen suffers from congestive heart failure, allergies, and asthma and has been hospitalized with pneumonia. She still manages to manage the house and cooks good meals for her family. Ray is a help around the house and yard; grandson Jeremy lives with them and helps with driving and running errands

Ed still has an active interest in sports and follows teams on TV and always attends his grandchildren's games. Now, when he is able, he goes to great-grandchildren's football games and their high school plays and choral concerts. He is proud of his children, who have done well in their careers and of grandson Ben who is studying medicine and great-grandson Justin will do so in the fall. Christopher, the oldest grandson was a star football player in high school and college and is now a coach and teacher in a Phoenix-area high school.

His granddaughter Kristi and her three children lived with Ed and Carmen. They enjoyed having the youngsters with them. Kristi, however, diagnosed as bipolar, had many emotional issues, which led to the courts taking custody of the children. Ed and Carmen were named guardians, but because of their poor health and age, Tomi, Kristi's sister, was awarded custody and later adopted the children into her family of three boys. Unfortunately, Kristi became addicted to drugs, overdosed, and died in spring 2019.

Ed and Carmen mourn Kristi's passing and wonder if they could have done more to help the troubled young woman but are grateful that her children are healthy and doing well in school.

Ed has always enjoyed art and has an untrained skill in sketching and drawing. He thinks this is an inherited talent, because he had uncles who were artists and Rose was a gifted painter. When in California, she did watercolors and won prizes in juried shows and sold her art. He doesn't expect to do as well as she did, but it gives him a great deal of satisfaction and pleasure and takes his mind off his disabilities.

Sometimes he and Carmen go to bingo with son Ray. The first time Ed went he won $7,000 and thought what an easy way to make money, but of course that only happened once. He likes playing roulette at one of the local casinos and stays even—doesn't lose too much nor win big jackpots. "I think it's the challenge of the game that I accept as I've done all my life. I've never been afraid of tackling new experiences and opportunities or taking chances. The result has not always been a good, but if I'm able, I'll keep trying.

"I am proud that I beat alcoholism," he states and realizes that he is one of thousands of Native Americans who have had a problem with alcohol since white traders first introduced it to the tribes. Native Americans did not have centuries of alcohol exposure behind them as Europeans did and they have little tolerance to it. Binge drinking was how the first Indians used alcohol; it reflected how nomadic tribes consumed food. When there was plenty, one ate it all, for no one knew when there would be another full plate. But Ed knows that is not an excuse for his years of being a drunk.

As of this writing Edward James Driving Hawk is eighty-four years old. Virginia says they have a longevity gene, inherited from their great-great-grandfather Howe, who lived to be one hundred and one. His daughter died one month short of her one hundredth birthday, as did their mother Rose. The last time Ed saw his mother was in 2003 when she came to Arizona to celebrate her ninetieth birthday. "I was so glad she came, because I can no longer travel, and I regret more than anything that I never saw her again.

"So," Ed reflects, "I expect to be here a while longer even though I live with pain and there are times when I want to ride off into the sunset, to let go and move into that place of light, warmth, and safety to join my ancestors. I'm ready, but I guess it isn't time."

NOTES

1. Sonny

1. Sneve, *That They May Have Life.*
2. Haskell Indian Nations University, "School History."
3. Sneve, *That They May Have Life.*
4. Dawes Act (1887).

4. Vietnam

1. Meacham, "A Year That Made the Present Seem Tranquil," 20.
2. American Cancer Society, "Agent Orange and Cancer Risk."
3. Alcoholics Anonymous.

5. Wakinyan Cangleska

1. Ward, "Remembering the Wounded Knee Occupation."
2. Robinson, *Doane Robinson's Encyclopedia of South Dakota.*
3. Wikipedia, "Leonard Crow Dog."
4. Dawes Act (1887).
5. Gilio-Whitaker, "The History Behind the Cobell Case."
6. United Sioux Tribes.
7. Larson, "The Story of a Dinosaur Named Sue."
8. Stout, "Congressman Faces Felony Charge."
9. Driving Hawk, "A National Indian Leader Summons Support for Political Unity."
10. *Encyclopaedia Britannica,* "Native American Church."

6. Too Strong to Be Broken

1. Burke, "What is Indian Preference?"
2. Lawson, *Dammed Indians Revisited.*
3. Federal Bureau of Prisons, "FCI Coleman Medium."

BIBLIOGRAPHY

Alcoholics Anonymous, https://aa.org/.

American Addiction Centers, accessed 2018, www.recovery.org.

American Cancer Society, "Agent Orange and Cancer Risk," accessed 2018, www.cancer.org/cancer/cancer-causes/agent-orange-and -cancer.html.

Burke, Lea Anne, "What is Indian Preference?," the Native Procurement Technical Assistance Center, accessed 2018, https://www .nativeptac.org/what-is-indian-preference/ (site discontinued).

Driving Hawk, Ed, "A National Indian Leader Summons Support for Political Unity: An Interview with Ed Driving Hawk," *American Indian Journal of the Institute for the Development of Indian Law 5*, no. 12 (December 1979): 18–22.

Encyclopaedia Britannica online, "Native American Church," www .britannica.com/topic/Native-American-Church.

Federal Bureau of Prisons, "FCI Coleman Medium," accessed 2018. www.bop.gov/locations/institutions/com/.

Gilio-Whitaker, Dina, "The History Behind the Cobell Case," *ThoughtCo*, updated March 18, 2017, www.thoughtco.com/history-behind-the -cobell-case-4082499.

Haskell Indian Nations University, "School History," accessed 2018, haskell.edu/about/history/.

Larson, Neal L., "The Story of a Dinosaur Named Sue," Black Hills Institute of Geological Research, Inc., updated May 18, 2000, www.bhigr.com/pages/info/info_sue.htm.

Lawson, Michael L., *Dammed Indians Revisited: The Continuing History of the Pick-Sloan Plan and the Missouri River Sioux.* Pierre SD: South Dakota State Historical Society Press, 2009.

Meacham, Jon, "A Year That Made the Present Seem Tranquil," *Time*, January 29, 2018.

Our Documents, "Dawes Act (1887)," accessed 2018, www.ourdocuments
.gov/doc.php?flash=true&doc=50.

Robinson, Doane, *Doane Robinson's Encyclopedia of South Dakota*. Pierre
SD: printed by the author, 1925.

Sneve, Virginia Driving Hawk, *Completing the Circle*. Lincoln: University of Nebraska Press, 1995.

———. *That They May Have Life: The Episcopal Church in South Dakota
1859–1976*. New York: Seabury Press, 1977.

Stout, David, "Congressman Faces Felony Charge in Fatal Accident,"
New York Times, August 29, 2003, www.nytimes.com/2003/08/29
/politics/congressman-faces-felony-charge-in-fatal-accident.html.

United Sioux Tribes of South Dakota Development Corporation, www
.unitedsiouxtribes.org.

U.S. Department of the Interior, Bureau of Indian Affairs, "Letter to
IIM Account Holders," Rosebud Agency, Rosebud SD. September 30, 1883.

U.S. Department of the Interior, Bureau of Indian Affairs, Rosebud
Reservation, www.bia.gov/regional-offices/great-plains/south
-dakota/rosebud-agency.

U.S. Government Publishing Office, "Code of Federal Regulations,"
www.govinfo.gov/help/cfr.

Ward, Brian, "Remembering the Wounded Knee Occupation," *Socialist Worker*, socialistworker.org/2013/02/27/remembering-the
-wounded-knee-occupation.

Wikipedia, "Leonard Crow Dog," last updated December 18, 2019,
https://en.wikipedia.org/wiki/Leonard_Crow_Dog.

In the American Indian Lives series

Essie's Story: The Life and Legacy of a Shoshone Teacher
By Esther Burnett Horne and Sally McBeth

Song of Rita Joe: Autobiography of a Mi'kmaq Poet
By Rita Joe

Viet Cong at Wounded Knee: The Trail of a Blackfeet Activist
By Woody Kipp

Catch Colt
By Sidner J. Larson

Alanis Obomsawin: The Vision of a Native Filmmaker
By Randolph Lewis

Alex Posey: Creek Poet, Journalist, and Humorist
By Daniel F. Littlefield Jr.

The Turtle's Beating Heart: One Family's Story of Lenape Survival
By Denise Low

First to Fight
By Henry Mihesuah
Edited by Devon Abbott Mihesuah

Mourning Dove: A Salishan Autobiography
Edited by Jay Miller

I'll Go and Do More: Annie Dodge Wauneka, Navajo Leader and Activist
By Carolyn Niethammer

Tales of the Old Indian Territory and Essays on the Indian Condition
By John Milton Oskison
Edited by Lionel Larré

Elias Cornelius Boudinot: A Life on the Cherokee Border
By James W. Parins

John Rollin Ridge: His Life and Works
By James W. Parins

Singing an Indian Song: A Biography of D'Arcy McNickle
By Dorothy R. Parker

Crashing Thunder: The Autobiography of an American Indian
Edited by Paul Radin

Turtle Lung Woman's Granddaughter
By Delphine Red Shirt and Lone Woman

Telling a Good One: The Process of a Native American Collaborative Biography
By Theodore Rios and Kathleen Mullen Sands

Out of the Crazywoods
By Cheryl Savageau

William W. Warren: The Life, Letters, and Times of an Ojibwe Leader
By Theresa M. Schenck

Sacred Feathers: The Reverend Peter Jones (Kahkewaquonaby)
and the Mississauga Indians
By Donald B. Smith

Grandmother's Grandchild: My Crow Indian Life
By Alma Hogan Snell
Edited by Becky Matthews
Foreword by Peter Nabokov

No One Ever Asked Me: The World War II Memoirs of an Omaha Indian Soldier
By Hollis D. Stabler
Edited by Victoria Smith

Blue Jacket: Warrior of the Shawnees
By John Sugden

Muscogee Daughter: My Sojourn to the Miss America Pageant
By Susan Supernaw
Foreword by Geary Hobson

I Tell You Now: Autobiographical Essays by Native American Writers
Edited by Brian Swann and Arnold Krupat

Postindian Conversations
By Gerald Vizenor and A. Robert Lee

Chainbreaker: The Revolutionary War Memoirs of Governor Blacksnake
As told to Benjamin Williams
Edited by Thomas S. Abler

Standing in the Light: A Lakota Way of Seeing
By Severt Young Bear and R. D. Theisz

Sarah Winnemucca
By Sally Zanjani

To order or obtain more information on these or other University of
Nebraska Press titles, visit nebraskapress.unl.edu.